HUPERETES

(AN UNDER-ROWER)

Available Books by Dr. Dennis Sempebwa

- *Surrounding Yourself with the Right People*
- *The Substance of Things Hoped For*
- *Timeless Truths — 300 Enduring Proverbs for Our Generation*
- *Deadly Distractions — Overcoming Life's Obstacles to Success*
- *Apostle Ruth Peterson — A Legacy of Love*
- *Perfectly Broken — Stories from the Potter's Wheel*
- *You Have a Dream: Proven Keys to Achieving Your Divine Destiny*
- *Dream Busters*
- *Huperetes — The Heart of a Minister*

HUPERETES
(AN UNDER-ROWER)
THE HEART OF A MINISTER

DR. DENNIS D. SEMPEBWA

Published by Eagle's Wings Press.

Publishing services by:
EVANGELISTA MEDIA & CONSULTING
Via Maiella, 1 66020 San Giovanni Teatino (CH) – Italy
publisher@evangelistamedia.com
www.evangelistamedia.com

For Worldwide Distribution, Printed in the USA

1 2 3 4 5 6 / 23 22 21 20

Dedication

To all who tirelessly toil in God's harvest fields around the world.

Acknowledgments

My precious wife, Ingrid. Thank you for loving me, nurturing our amazing chocolates—Adam, Abigail, Caleb, Judah, and Elijah—and for traveling this often-treacherous journey with me.

My precious mother, Deborah, my brothers and sisters— I love you all.

A shout out to the most dedicated administrator, armor-bearer, accountant, and road manager anywhere in the world, Lisa Romesburg. You and Dean are amazing gifts to the Sempebwas, our ministries, and the nations.

To my dedicated transcriber Irina Schinkelshoek. You are a godsend!

Special thanks to the Humphreys, the Valencianos, the Schroeders, and all our teams both in the USA and around the world. Thank you for walking with us. It is a great honor to serve with you all.

Let a man so account of us, as of the ministers of Christ, and stewards of the mysteries of God.

—1 Corinthians 4:1

What Other Leaders Say

If you feel God calling you into ministry, are just starting out in ministry, or have been in the ministry for many years, you will benefit from reading *Huperetes*. I can say that because I have been in ministry for over four decades, and Dr. Dennis Sempebwa covers all the challenges I have faced! This book reminds us that what we are experiencing is not unusual, and we are not alone. God is with us, and many have gone through what we are going through. Read and be encouraged!

Dr. Roberts Liardon
President | Roberts Liardon Ministries
Lead Pastor | Embassy International Church
USA

I greatly appreciate what Dennis covers in the pages of this book. *Huperetes* helps us rediscover or reestablish why we do what we do, and who we do it for. Dennis encourages us to understand we are "stewards of the mysteries of God," and that these glorious life-giving truths, anointings, positions and responsibilities have been entrusted to us in our present generation to bring to pass God's purpose and make Him—not us—known. These pages will help define the difference between striving to be successful and endeavoring to be faithful. These truths allow us to speak to the Timothys in our lives. These pages will help men and women protect generational ministry—where we understand legacy is about the continued and expanding purpose of God from generation to generation and not the expansion of our reputation. *Huperetes* will help develop character and establish your roots, which will determine your fruit and the fruit which will remain. Be enriched and established in these pages that will help bring you to the place where you hear, "Well done good and faithful servant."

Dr. Paul Chase
Lead Pastor & Founder | New Life Churches
Philippines

In this concise and insightful volume, Dr. Dennis has done what he does best, taken a potentially complex matter and broken it down into simple, comprehensible portions that make *Huperetes* a timely handbook and guide for Christian ministry today. He writes for a global audience that could understandably be presumed in millions, yet he cultivates an appropriately personal tone that succeeds in making the book compellingly applicable to an audience of one! And while reading the last chapter, the great hymn of the church, composed by Knowles Shaw in 1874, replayed in my mind, leading me back to Psalm 126:6 – *"He who goes forth and weeps, bearing precious seed to sow, shall come home again with rejoicing, bringing his grain sheaves with him"* (MEV © 2014). Thank you, my brother and friend, Dr. Dennis. This is timely!

Bishop Dr. Joshua HK Banda, PhD
Overseer/Senior Pastor | Northmead Assembly of God
Lusaka, Zambia
President | Pentecostal Assemblies of Africa (PAOA)
Southern Africa Region

While Dr. Dennis Sempebwa's latest book, *Huperetes*, is epic in its unveiled treasure, it has proven guidelines gleaned from his 40 years of global experience and is about to bring you to the genesis of your purpose. Realize this, your purpose predates your conception. You are just a choice away from your new beginning—a new you—a ministry and purpose worthy of your potential. When you are serious about change, you don't need a NEW YEAR—you just need a NEW MOMENT. This narrative penned in these pages is about to bring you to this moment! I salute you Dennis, my lifelong friend and co-laborer in the nations, for the treasure that is proclaimed and for those seeded with these thoughts trumpeted.

Dr. Mike Francen
President | Francen World Outreach
USA

Anyone who has seen the movie *Ben Hur* would not easily forget the picture of Charles Heston playing the protagonist in that fierce battle that was also his redemption. Chained to the bottom of the Roman charging vessel, *Ben Hur* slavishly follows the pounding beats along with other slaves propelling the vessel to almost certain death. That picture is certainly a far cry from the glamour of a modern-day megachurch preacher pounding on his pulpit preaching away to a captivated crowd who look to him as the spokesperson of God. These are two very different pictures of a leader! Yet very true to the life of a minister of the gospel. With his story-telling style and African charm, Dr. Dennis guides his readers through the seven tests of leadership. The idea of an under-rower is definitely going to challenge an aspiring preacher to examine his stewardship of God's gifts to him as revealed through the tests a servant of God must go through. If you have already a mental picture of what a leader looks like, *Huperetes* may give you a godly makeover. Highly recommended!

Rev. Dr. John Kuo
Lead Pastor | Wu Chang Church
Taiwan

Dr. Dennis Sempebwa is a very gifted writer. His new book, *Huperetes*, is carrying a fresh message; and most importantly, a very necessary one. Our generation needs more servants to disciple the world, and this book is a special tool for the young servants as well as for the experienced ones. Dr. Sempebwa introduces in his book some of the Bible's heroes; but not only that, Dennis with much talent clarifies what was the secret of their great achievements. *Huperetes* is not just a must read, it needs to be put into practice... I do hope that *Huperetes* will be translated in the Romanian language because I am totally convinced that the impact will be of an apostolic magnitude.

Dr. Buni Cocar
Author & Evangelist
Lead Pastor | Maranatha Romanian Church
Romania

So many of us want to be used by God, to have His heart, but our perspective has been influenced by what the world teaches us. Because we sons of Adam, want to become great, He became small; because we aspire for distinction, He humbled Himself; because we want to rule, He came to serve. A believer in the Lord Jesus who maintains high spiritual standards may find himself following His Master on the pathway. *Huperetes* is a book that will challenge the status quo of ministers in this new millennium.

This book is calling us back to our basics. Thank you, son, for this gift to the Body of Christ. We are proud of you!

Drs. Kurt and Mary Alice Schroeder
Lead Pastors | The Goodnews Center
USA

What a beautiful read! When I opened this script, I sort of braced myself for a task. Instead I found myself on an effortless, stroll through one of the most readable scripts I have read in a long time. And I read through in one sitting on a Sunday morning before heading out to church. I should have known though because, "profoundly educational" and yet "simple and to the point" is the summary of how Dr. Dennis speaks, writes and ministers. As I put the script down, I felt strangely warm, because I instantly recognized everything that I read as familiar, yet I could have never put it so well myself. *Huperetes* is a timely and powerful resource and tool in reminding and challenging ministers around the world what true ministry looks like. Thank you, Dennis, for distilling many years of exposure to the best and worst examples and experiences of ministry models around the world into this little treasury of truth and wisdom.

Pastor Lincoln Kasirye
Lead Pastor | Liberty Christian Fellowship
UK

This book is a must-read for those who are starting in the ministry and to those who need to be reminded of what God called them to do. Ministry is not about glamour or fame. It is not easy nor comfortable. Ministry is servanthood and sacrifice. *Huperetes* will challenge you to do the ministry Jesus' way. May you receive the revelation that this book seeks to offer. May you be transformed to become a true servant of Christ.

Rev. Bishop Timmy Benedict S. Lao Uy
Regional Overseer | Word for the World Christian Fellowship
Lead Pastor | WWCF – Cebu
Philippines

Huperetes defines the integral path to the journey of a minister whose heart beats for purpose beyond their gifting, and their part in the Great Commission beyond present opportunities.

Apostle Grace Lubega
Lead Pastor | Phaneroo Ministries International
Uganda

I have come to know Dr. Dennis Sempebwa as the Lord has given us the opportunities to serve together in several countries. I am amazed at the grace and faith that the Lord has given this genuine man of God. When he speaks, I hear the heart of a tested man; a humble man—a huperetes—who knows his place in the Kingdom of God. *Huperetes* will produce the discomfort that the voice of the Holy Spirit produces when He speaks to the most intimate part of our hearts. It is not a book for those who want triumph, success, or the lights of human flattery. It is a book for those who want to let God mold their lives to be simple servants who seek the glory of God. When I see what is going on in ministry today, I ask myself: Are we really ready for God's Kingdom to come? This is what this book is about: Making Jesus Lord, making Jesus the center. My prayer is that by reading *Huperetes*, you will decode the urgent message contained in it.

Pastor Armando Sánchez
Lead Pastor | Centro Cristiano Restauración Familiar
Spain

As a minister for over 30 years, I can confidently say that *Huperetes* is a must read. Because it displays a deep insight into the call to ministry, I consider it a manual, one that ought to be kept close. Dr. Dennis parallels the call to ministry to that of the under-rower, who holds his position for a lifetime. For me, ministry is just that, and I am encouraged (refueled) to continue my journey with the valuable insight and tools contained in this manual. For those who are about to answer the call to Kingdom service, and to some of us who have been doing this for decades, I encourage you to read with eyes, minds and hearts wide open as this book speaks to all aspects of the journey of ministry. Read it, pass it on, and read it again. Thank you, Dr. Dennis.

Pastor Ruth Pipersburgh
Lead Pastor | Trinity Assembly of God Church
Founder | The Reformation Team
Belize

I vividly remember the first time I heard Dr. Dennis teach *Huperetes* in Kampala, Uganda. He had us build a life-sized boat to illustrate the often-brutal nature of the call of God. As he sat in that boat and started rowing, an awe fell upon the hundreds of ministers in that auditorium. I wished someone had taught me as a *huperetes* 25 years ago when I first volunteered to serve. After leading missions campaigns in 30 nations from the mud huts in Pokot, Kenya, to the ritzy mansions in Orange County, California, I am once again compelled to ask this sobering question: "Am I really a servant?" I have been honored to serve alongside Dr. Dennis and Ingrid for the last decade. He lives the truths captured in this book. *Huperetes* will make you look at your heart. It is a must-read for anyone who has heeded the glorious invitation to serve Jesus Christ.

Lisa Romesburg
Chief Operating Officer | Eagle's Wings International
Dean of Students | THE 300
USA

The global meteoric rise of Limit X, a Ugandan Gospel group of which Dennis Sempebwa was a part, happened around the end of our high school and early college years. In our eyes, these guys were legends—still are. So when Dennis and his Eagle's Wings team were coming to visit Worship Harvest for the first time, I wasn't so sure we had what it takes to host "The Legend." Well, as it turned out, they were all very simple, humble, down to earth people who only sought to serve. It's been wonderful serving together these past few years. In this book, Dr. Dennis takes the very principles of ministry he lives by and distills them for us to remember who, how and why we serve. I highly recommend *Huperetes* to every minister and believer.

Pastor Moses Mukisa
Lead Pastor | Worship Harvest
Uganda

Dr. Dennis Sempebwa has been a close friend and ministry associate for over 20 years. In a world where posturing, deceitfulness, and hubris are the order of the day, he brings us back to the place where serving the Lord is an honorable call with candor, integrity, and humility. His experiences captured in this book bring to light some of the most important issues facing ministry practitioners today. I have been touched by some of the insights here and have learned some valuable lessons. Our generation will be richer for these truths captured here.

Dr. Pete Odera
Musician & Author
Lead Pastor | The Waterbrook Church
Kenya

Having known Dr. Dennis now for over 25 years I can unequiv-ocally say that he is indeed a soldier of the cross of Jesus Christ and has been all these years. While he has served under many titles, the one common ground of his entire ministry has been that of a servant! With promotion and elevation through God's calling upon his life, he has done what only a few have done, remain humble through the process of promotion. This is what qualifies him to author this excellent book, *Huperetes*, which means under-rower! As you sit to read this incredible reflection of God's government, buckle up for it may mess up some of your previous training, as we see Jesus calling us to servanthood and not necessarily leadership positioning. The last shall be first! Promotion in God's economy comes through serving faithfully which is why God has entrusted the nations to my friend, Dr. Dennis Sempebwa!

Pastor Gary Cavalier,
Lead Pastor | Life Church
Executive Director | Castaway Ministries
USA

I encountered Dr. Dennis growing up as a child watching him and his band of brothers minister all over the world through the group Limit X. I met him nearly 20 years later in Nairobi at the Fearless summit at Mavuno church and I have had the privilege of connecting with him. He absolutely has a heart for the next generation and is a true ambassador for the gospel. *Huperetes* is a throwback to the calling to carrying our cross, something that I believe has been lost in many of our churches today due to the glamorization of ministry that has prevented many from being resilient in their pursuit of obedience to what God is calling them to. This book will bring us back to the place of genuine calling and sacrifice and redefine what true success in ministry really means, a distinction between what is true and what is false…birthing the next generation of true leaders to advance the Kingdom of God.

Michael Obbo Onen
Actor, Singer/Songwriter
Lead Pastor | Mavuno Church Kampala
Team Leader | Mavuno Church
Uganda

Ministry is not rosy because it is service, and service is inconvenient. Dr. Dennis just nailed it. *Huperetes* is brief and simple, catchy, compelling, and driving. You cannot read Dr. Dennis's *Huperetes* and not want to invite him to your congregation. He shares experience plus reality for the minister. This book is the perfect, ageless Ministers' Manual for fulfilling the great commission around the world. It is the book for every genuine minister and ministry but beyond that, it can apply to all aspects of human life and business.

Pastor Daddy-Ken A. Bitere
Lead Coach & CEO | Daddy-Ken Ministries International
Lead Pastor | The Refined People's Assembly
Nigeria

In this must-read book, Dr. Dennis asserts what we as Christians truly are "servants." It brings to light what a servant is by breaking down our pride to help us to truly give glory to Jesus, where it truly belongs. I have known Dr. Dennis for years and have learned so much from him. I have seen his heart and admire his humbleness as a servant of God. I have witnessed him live out this book as being a under-rower in the faith of Christ! I highly recommend this book to new and old believers in the faith.

You will be challenged as you examine your heart and excited as you take your place as a *Huperetes*.

Pastor Frank Hernandez
Lead Pastor | Kingdom Living Church
USA

In this age, we have lost the quintessence of a true minister of Christ and have rebranded it to suit our own selfish needs. For many of us, ministry is glitziness and if it's not, then God is not with us and we are left feeling defeated. Increasingly, we think that ministry is what happens on our colorfully lit stages under the glare of cameras, yet true ministry is a product of authentic servanthood which takes place in obscurity behind the scenes. In *Huperetes*, Dr. Dennis takes us back to the Bible truth and juxtaposes our warped image of a minister with prominent ministers in the Bible to show us how far we have drifted. He awakens us to the fact that what drives a car is not what is plainly visible but what lies underneath the hood—and this is true with ministry. Having been challenged by this great book, I highly recommend it for anyone who is serious about pleasing God with the way they serve Him and His people.

Pastor Reuben Chief Guma
Lead Pastor | Shiloh Tabernacle
UK

The passion of Christianity is that I deliberately sign away my own rights and become a bond-slave of Jesus Christ. Until I do that, I do not begin to be a minister of God. This is necessary because the Master bought us all with a price; and as His own, He inputted His divine nature into us to enable us surrender completely to Him in service. However, as humans, some costs are to be incurred. This is the focus of this book. *Huperetes* is so relevant for Africa today because most ministers forget that serving God is not free. They go ahead the easy way creating pollution and corruption in the spiritual atmosphere. The relevance of this book cannot be contested as I presume that readers will understand better their responsibilities toward effective service to God. It is a book for all those involved in the 5-fold ministry of the Lord Jesus Christ.

Pastor James O. Chuku
Lead Pastor | Royal House of Grace International Church
Nigeria

Dr. Dennis D. Sempebwa uses the Greek word *Huperetes* in the title of his book, which literally means "an under-rower," as a way to define the biblical role of a minister. The word is used to signify extreme lowliness and a position of subordination or submission. In *Huperetes*, he defines and dissects the biblical term "minister." What should a biblical minister be in today's culture that is influenced by mega churches and its celebrity pastors. In this book, Dr. Sempebwa breaks down the real minister's role and responsibilities that is so needed in today's church. More than ever today we need authentic ministers to servant-lead God's church. Our culture is crying out for real ministers of the Word and Dr. Sempebwa has done an excellent job of breaking down the biblical role of minister in *Huperetes*. A must-read for all who want to serve in God's church and carry the title minister!

Pastor Mark Stevens
Executive Pastor | Rock Church
USA

Masterful storyteller, Dr. Dennis brings real-life examples that demystifies the "glamour" of ministry and restores our understanding of the powerful link between spiritual authority and what "Normal" is for a true servant of God. He expertly discerns the tests that make or break any minister of the gospel. The class is set, exams hot off the press. Now the teacher waits for the students to come and pass the tests. Each of us must face the tests or risk never graduating from the exam room. Those who study diligently the principles of *Huperetes* will pass and succeed the way Jesus wanted us to. In an age where "inconvenience" and "endurance" are curse words to the general public, *Huperetes* finds the servant's true north, and boldly points the way and walks with you to the end. Pack your bags, say goodbye to what you have known, and embrace your God-given destiny as you learn how to hold your oar and row.

Pastor Jesse Millar
Missionary & International Pastor | Beza International
Ethiopia

Contents

Prologue

What is ministry? Let's first look at the foundational text for the thesis of this book:

> *Let a man so account of us, as of the ministers of Christ, and stewards of the mysteries of God* (1 Corinthians 4:1).

"*...ministers of Christ...*" Hmmm...fascinating that Paul chooses to use the word *"ministers."* To understand the weight of this designation, let's look at the word in Greek, *huperetes[1]*, which literally means "an under-rower." The word is used to signify extreme lowliness and deep vassalage, which is a position of subordination or submission.

If you have watched the Hollywood blockbuster movie *Ben Hur*, there is a scene where slaves are rowing a large galley ship, not from the top deck like we are used to seeing, but from the lowest level of the ship. Their task was to move the ship, like a human engine. Their entire job description was to row the ship no matter what. All they did, night and day was row, row, row, or *hupereteo*, through calm and rough seas. *A huperetes* and his many coworkers were often confined to their benches with large chains, in case they wanted to escape.

Paul intentionally uses *huperetes* to define ministry. No matter how convention is trying to distort its true meaning, authentic ministry is not: easy; comfortable; glamorous; autonomous; predictable; or temporary. Let's look more closely at each of these descriptions of what ministry is not.

1. Ministry is not easy.

A young man passionately claims he is ready to serve God. So I tell him, "Great, please be here at 6 a.m. sharp next Sunday to help us set up for the services."

"What?" he protests. "That's too early. Do you have something else I can do? I'm just not a morning person!"

Right then I knew he wasn't ready. There is no such a thing as easy ministry. As *huperetes*', we work long hours, often with difficult bench-mates, under difficult circumstances.

2. Ministry is not comfortable.

I remember bringing a team of American missionaries home to Uganda with me a few years ago. After twenty-four hours of flying, we were all understandably exhausted. After waiting for over an hour for our bags after landing in the Entebbe airport, our hosts broke the news to the team, "Well, get comfortable. We have two hours of driving into the city." I could see the anxiety on the missionaries' faces. The worst was not yet over.

When we arrived at the hotel, our room reservations had been dropped, so we couldn't check in for another couple of hours.

By now, the missionaries were frazzled. Finally, I was relieved to have everyone in their rooms—until the phone calls began:

"My bed is uncomfortable, Dr. Dennis. I have back problems."

"I can't sleep on this pillow."

"Do you think they can get me a bottle of purified water?"

"The crickets are too loud. I can't sleep."

Suddenly I realized that my team was ill-prepared for global missions. They wanted to replicate the comforts of home in a third world country. My team had missed a key truth that authentic ministry is not comfortable.

3. Ministry is not glamorous.

A few years ago, I was hosted by a megachurch pastor for a large regional conference. As we made our way to the auditorium from his office, a woman broke through his security perimeter and ran straight into his arms, weeping uncontrollably. Her son had just died. The pastor was visibly irritated as he gently pushed her away.

When we got to our seats in the reserved front section, he called his head of security and sternly chided him, "Look at this," pointing to a smudge on his suit, "This is a $3,000 Brioni suit. It's all messed up now because you failed to do your job. Why did you let that woman through?"

I was mortified. I thought, *I would boldly wear the tear-stained suit showing that I cared for the grieving mother. In fact, I would have the church pray for her right now.*

Regardless what some modern-day televangelists or megachurch pastors portray, ministry is not about private jets, lavish vacations, large estates, or fame. In other words, ministry is not where you come to get rich, powerful, or influential. On the contrary, it is where you come to die to yourself. You are a *huperetes!*

4. Ministry is not autonomous.

When God first calls us, we are often doubted. Sometimes, even our friends don't think we have what it takes to obey God's call for our lives. So we unwittingly develop a defensive mechanism to protect us from critics. We decide its safer to row alone. One pastor said to me, "Dennis, ministry would be so fun if it were not for all these messed up people!" Well, ministry is the people business. We get to run with friends, do life with others because it's not a solo sport. We don't get to do it alone. We don't get to do it our way. We need company. It is the only way we get to effectively serve, to *hupereteo*.

5. Ministry is not predictable.

"I hate schedule changes," cried the one executive pastor. "I need people to show up when they said they would and for things to fall in place as planned…or I am ready to quit doing this!" Sounds like the brother wanted to manage a well-oiled business outfit. Not ministry!

Real ministry is not predictable, nor can it really be. Nobody gives you the plan because we don't know the plan. This is God's work, remember? Servants of the Lord must show up each day, ready to obey God's marching orders whether they like them or not. They don't get to ask, "Hmmm…Jesus, can I have a better schedule, please? These hours don't work for me!" or, "This doesn't fit my personality," or "I'm not comfortable with this."

6. Ministry is not temporary.

Ministry is a permanent venture. When we answer God's call, He will immediately rearrange us and ultimately change us. We don't get to retire. Indeed, we might step down from a role, but the notion that we just stop because we are too old or too tired is simply not an option. In fact, the more experienced we are, the richer we become. Remember, a *huperetes* served in the bottom bowels of those ships for a lifetime. There was no quitting. There was no retirement. They rowed until they died!

Wow Dennis, ministry sounds intense, you might think. Yes, it is. And it is supposed to be. Ministry is not for the timid or faint of heart; but even still, Paul calls it a *"high calling"* (Philippians 3:14).

I have been in ministry for forty years now. I have served in worship ministry, youth ministry, street ministry, intercession ministry, pastoral ministry, prophetic ministry, and apostolic ministry. My journey has gifted me with 10,000 stories of courageous ministers who have made bold sacrifices and given everything to champion the cause of Christ.

Conversely, I have also seen greedy charlatans, selfish manipulators, and shameless opportunists whose singular objective was to fleece the sheep for personal gain—wolves in sheep's clothing.

Rather than articulate keys to effective ministry or offer textbook or theological truisms for clergy, allow me to engage you from a different perspective in this brief book.

I invite you to consider what I call the *seven tests of servanthood— each is a chapter title.*

Why tests? Paul writes:

Examine yourselves to see whether you are in the faith; test yourselves. Do you not realize that Christ Jesus is in you—unless, of course, you fail the test? (2 Corinthians 13:5 NIV)

Powerful thought, right? So, Paul has a suggestion for us. You think you are in the faith? Then test yourself. If you fail the test, then you are basically fake. Sounds harsh? Maybe. Well, read Paul's sobering question: *"Do you not realize that Christ Jesus is in you—unless, of course, you fail the test?"*

Why servanthood and not leadership? Check out Jesus' admonition to His disciples:

Sitting down [to teach], He called the twelve [disciples] and said to them, "If anyone wants to be first, he must be last of all [in importance] and a servant of all" (Mark 9:35 AMP).

This is huge!

Jesus is saying that being on top comes from reaching for the bottom. Ministry is not so much about leading but serving. This is the foundation for all authentic ministry—serving.

Let's get right into it with discussing the first test, The Test of Faith—followed by The Test of Conviction; The Test of Isolation; The Test of Servanthood; The Test of Reputation; The Test of Time; and The Test of Success.

Endnote

1. The NAS New Testament Greek Lexicon, Strong's #5257.

CHAPTER 1

The Test of Faith

Will you row without a game plan?

Now the Lord had said unto Abram, "Get thee out of thy country, and from thy kindred, and from thy father's house, unto a land that I will shew thee" (Genesis 12:1 KJV).

The New King James version of the Bible says it this way:

Now the Lord had said to Abram: "Get out of your country, from your family and from your father's house, to a land that I will show you" (Genesis 12:1 NKJV).

This verse in Genesis 12 marks the beginning of what would be the most significant ministry in the history of the earth, besides the ministry of Christ, of course. Here is why:

In your seed all the nations of the earth shall be blessed, because you have obeyed My voice (Genesis 22:18 NKJV).

Great, right? So, Abraham's ministry could lead to a global blessing. Yes! *Everyone* on earth would be blessed because of it.

To some, the instruction seems simple, maybe even cool. Moving to a new town can be exciting, right? Well, not for Abram. He was settled in a place called Haran, which means "perched" in Hebrew. His father and father's father had dwelt there for generations.

Allow me to paraphrase God's proposal:

"Hey Abram…I want to do something really powerful with your life, so here is the deal: get up and leave your country, your family, your relatives…really your identity…and prepare to go somewhere I will show you. In other words—leave this safety net for Me and I will bless you."

Now, does that sound even remotely reasonable to you? Of course not! Frankly speaking, it's a ridiculous instruction. Think about it. Abram was asked to say *yes* to a vague proposition to sojourn to an undisclosed destination.

Imagine Abram explaining the absurd instruction to his family:

"Hey guys, God almighty spoke to me today."

"No way…Yahweh spoke? Wow! What did He say?"

"Well, you won't believe this, but He asked me to do something that I can't quite figure out."

"Great, what's that?"

"Okay here goes…we are to tear down this tent dwelling and move away from here."

"What? But Abram, we belong here. This is our home! Where on earth would Jehovah want us to go?"

"Well...I'm afraid I really don't know where."

Imagine just how ludicrous and irresponsible that would have sounded.

Ministry begins with a deliberate divorcement from the cords that bind us to our worldly identity.

The good news is that Abram obeys and leaves his ancestral dwelling, although not immediately. He hangs out in Haran for another five years; and to make matters worse, Abram decides to take along his dad, Terah—which interestingly means "delayed" in Hebrew—and nephew, Lot, who would become a major problem later on.

THE INVITE

Like with Abram, all ministry begins with a seemingly ridiculous invitation.

I remember my invitation.

Shortly after my conversion on January 12, 1980, I joined the Redeemed Church of Christ in Kampala, Uganda. I vividly remember the day I heard about the street evangelism team. I had seen Christians witnessing on the street corners before. They seemed nutty and even cultish. They would get up on top of ant mounds on dusty road junctions and literally yell out their sins—sins that Jesus had washed away, they claimed. They would then break out into song. I liked the singing, but the whole thing was bizarre. The deep introvert in me couldn't understand why anyone would want to embarrass themselves like that. Could I be one of them?

Week after week I would hear testimonies of the works of Jesus on the streets. I felt the Holy Spirit drawing me to serve God on the street evangelism team. I had never spoken in public and didn't think I could articulate any kind of testimony, nor did I even think I really had one. See, I had been a "good boy" all my life. Didn't drink, chase girls, smoke, or anything like that. That was my first *Test of Faith*. The Lord was asking me, "Dennis...will you allow Me to use you even when you don't have anything to say?" Like with Abram, God needed a response. I had to say *yes* before I knew what to say, or how to say it!

And that I did… I remember the first time I was called out to testify. The guy before me had just told everyone how Jesus saved him from witchcraft. The gal before him had just told us how she had slept with all the village leaders. Then I was up.

"I thank God for saving me too!" I sheepishly said, with my voice crackling from the nervousness.

"From what?" yelled the drunk right on the front row. My mind went blank. For a second there, I wished I hadn't been so good. I wish I had committed more sins so I would have a "better" testimony. I fumbled through the segment and quickly handed back the bull horn. I was mortified. *Never again...I will never do this again!*

Well I was back the following day, and the next day until I stopped freaking out. Eventually, I learned to appreciate that my testimony was Jesus had saved me from the brutal scars of worldliness that my friends struggled with. Bottom line is: it didn't matter whether I liked it or was comfortable with it. I was a *huperetes*.

And straightway Jesus constrained his disciples to get into a ship, and to go before him unto the other side, while he sent the multitudes away. And when he had sent the multitudes away, he went up into a mountain apart to pray: and when the evening was come, he was there alone. But the ship was now in the midst of the sea, tossed with waves: for the wind was contrary. And in the fourth watch of the night Jesus went unto them, walking on the sea. And when the disciples saw him walking on the sea, they were troubled, saying, It is a spirit; and they cried out for fear. But straightway Jesus spake unto them, saying, Be of good cheer; it is I; be not afraid. And Peter answered him and said, Lord, if it be thou, bid me come unto thee on the water (Matthew 14:22-28).

Let's stop for a moment and ponder Peter's crazy proposition. Remember, the disciples had just been hit with an unexpected storm. For hours, they had been struggling to keep their boat dry and afloat. They were barely hanging on—struggling for their lives. They saw what looked like Jesus, but they needed to make sure. Mister Outspoken Peter had an idea: "Hey Jesus, if it's really You out there, invite me to join you and we can walk out there together!"

Implicit in this rather crazy proposal must have also been this thought: *If I am totally off and this is some ghost and not You, Jesus, then I will certainly perish!*

Jesus probably thought, *Way to go, Peter. You really want to adventure with Me? Okay! Let's do this.*

So He said, "Come" (Matthew 14:29 NKJV).

In other words, Jesus was saying, "Step out of your boat and do crazy with Me!"

The boat represented:

- Familiar
- Safe
- Normal
- Predictable
- Reasonable

Jesus invites Peter to step off the bow into:

- Unfamiliar
- Dangerous
- Disruptive
- Unpredictable
- Unreasonable

Ministry involves a foggy invitation to go where you have never been.

I often hear people say, "Dr. Dennis, I know that God wants to use me, but I just do not know how. Please pray for me that He will show me His plans for my life." Sounds reasonable, right? Unfortunately, it's a misguided thought.

Contrary to popular charismatic theology, God does not share His plans with us. Remember we are talking about the God of the universe here—the Beginning and the End, the Omniscient God, the King of kings and Lord of lords. Do we honestly think we could fathom His thoughts? That He would say, "Okay, son, here is what is in My heart for you."

Friend, do we think ourselves more special than Abraham, the father of our faith? Because he didn't know the plan before he said yes, you will not know either. Remember, at the heart of the call to ministry is a crazy, wild, ridiculous invitation to walk into the fog of the unknown.

MY INVITATIONS

A few months after I joined the street evangelism ministry, I started feeling a draw to music. Our church didn't have modern musical instruments, so we played African drums called *nnankasi* and *ngalabi*. I was absolutely transfixed. One day, I asked the drummer to teach me.

"Where were you born?" he quizzed.

"Mukono, but have lived in Kampala's suburbs since I was a child," I said excitedly.

"Ahh…then this is not for you. You are a city boy and city boys don't play local drums."

I was devastated.

But thank God I didn't listen. I kept showing up before services and eventually started sitting right next to that drummer. One day he didn't show up. With thousands of people staring at me, I stepped right in and started serving in the worship ministry. As a result of my obedience, God completely revolutionized traditional praise and worship music throughout our nation.

But I felt God had more…

I started feeling drawn to the keyboards. Upon inquiry, the worship leader said, "Dennis, drummers cannot really play modern instruments. They stick to their genre…drums." Thank God I didn't listen. I taught myself to play the accordion, keyboards, and guitar. I ended up creating new fusions of African pop that drew thousands of young people to Christ. God used us to champion a new musical style that helped usher in a nationwide revival.

But I felt God had more…

I was drawn to singing, but my voice was untrained. My friends said, "Hey, musicians don't sing, y'know! Just keep playing…it's good enough!" Thank God I didn't listen. I learned to sing and even write songs. My friends and I formed an award-winning ensemble that released five CDs and broke records worldwide.

But I felt God had more…

After singing all around the world for seventeen years, I started to feel that familiar pull: "Dennis, get out of the boat. Come walk with Me! There is more to do." The Lord was telling me I would train leaders worldwide. But I hadn't even finished college. My father had passed away a month before I was to enroll in the only university in Uganda. Besides, I was safe. We were very famous and very successful. We were touching nations with our music. Why rock the boat?

What followed was something amazing. God gave me a voracious hunger for reading. I would "devour" three books a week. He led me to meet with the president of Life Christian University, who offered to scholarship me through my undergraduate journey.

Meanwhile, we were still singing weekly around the world. I would order multiple courses from the university and gobbled up every paragraph of information. I was hungry. I completed my Bachelor's degree, followed by my Master's, and eventually my first PhD—all in record time.

My friends would ask, "Dennis, why are you getting educated? Are you not happy with the success God has given you?" I didn't know why, but something inside my gut was saying, *There is coming a new season of your life for which you must prepare.* I completed my higher education and then accepted a position at a church, cofounding and leading a college program. The International College of Excellence would explode, spawning twenty-two extension campuses in multiple countries.

But I felt God had more…

At the time, I was learning about spiritual authority. I remember conferring with a man I greatly respected: "Sir, I really feel like God is stirring me up to launch out and do global ministry." I was excited. This man had been pivotal to my spiritual growth so I thought, *Surely, he is going to confirm the impression and bless me. This time, I won't have to step out alone.*

"Why would you do that?" he barked. "You have a future here. Your kids have a future here. You have a family to support. Well, let me ask you this: What exactly is God asking you to do, and how are you going to support your family doing it?"

I couldn't answer. I didn't know. Then he said something that haunted me for months: "Dennis, if you can't explain exactly what God is calling you to, then that is not God!"

I was devastated. I felt selfish and ungrateful. Indeed, we were touching the world. What more did I want? Out of respect, I obeyed him. He was my spiritual father.

But the rumblings remained. I started to fast and pray. "Lord, if this is You, confirm and I will step out!"

That weekend, I flew to Guatemala to preach in a conference. As soon as I stepped into the auditorium to prepare for my session, the speaker behind the podium stopped in the middle of his message and said, "Sir…this is the Word of the Lord to you: Whatever you are wrestling with is of Me. You are to step out and follow Me. I will bless you indeed!" Then he went on with his message.

I wept. That was my confirmation. I was to step away from this safe ministry environment and risk it all to serve God in the nations.

In August 1986, I resigned from the school and launched Eagle's Wings International (EWI). And the rest, as they say, is history. My spiritual father was wrong. I did not need to have a game plan to obey God. I have since authored books, pastored pastors of congregations, and ministered to millions of people in eighty countries.

But I felt God had more…

In January 2014, the Lord said to me, "Find My 300!" I didn't have a clue what that meant. Gideon is one of my favorite biblical heroes, but what did that have to do with EWI and our work in the nations? Six months later, He said again, "Dennis, find My 300. Upon this rock I will build My Church!" Well, that didn't make much sense at all. Why would God conflate Judges 7 with Matthew 16?

I told Ingrid and my team and left it alone.

Five years later, the Lord began to explain what He wanted us to do. We were to launch a Christocentric, multiethnic ministry training college that would make disciples of all nations. Without resources, we launched THE 300. Today, we train hundreds of ministers in dozens of countries.

But I feel God has more…

I am being invited into places where I am completely unprepared. I am being pushed to go swim in really deep waters as I take the message of the Cross to the darkest places of the earth. Am I scared? Of course! Naturally, I really want to swim in familiar waters…to keep doing what I know, what works. I can easily populate my ministry calendar with invitations for two years straight. I can just keep doing what I am comfortable doing.

But the Lord keeps saying, "No, son…there is more inside of you." In front of me is the next *Test of Faith*. Will I do it even if I don't know how? Will I say yes to something I do not even have a clue about? And I shall, by God's grace, pass this test. Will you?

God is not obligated to share His roadmap for us.

FOLLOW ME

As Jesus was walking beside the Sea of Galilee, he saw two brothers, Simon called Peter and his brother Andrew. They were casting a net into the lake, for they were fishermen (Matthew 4:18 NIV).

Imagine Peter and Andrew, preparing for a hard day ahead. They are fishermen. I can imagine Peter's wife bidding him farewell before he left the house that morning. We know he was married; and I am sure she fully expected him to return home with a good catch that evening like he had always done.

For thirty years, Jesus didn't do anything miraculous or particularly special. We don't have a record of any healings prior to the launch of His public ministry. As far as we know, He was a normal young man. Mary, His mama, could have told everyone what she knew. Simply stated, Jesus was God's Kid. Instead, she *"...kept all these things, and pondered them in her heart"* (Luke 2:19).

So Jesus is baptized by His cousin John the Baptist and BOOM! It all begins. God audibly declares His approval, but Jesus vanishes for more than a month. No one knows where He is until He suddenly strolls up to these two brothers that morning and says:

> *...Follow Me, and I will make you fishers of men* (Matthew 4:19 NKJV).

I am sure all kinds of thoughts crossed their minds. Follow You? Where? How? What was He inviting them to? Surely they needed to know, especially since Jesus hadn't really done anything of significance yet. But look what they did:

> *At once they left their nets and followed him* (Matthew 4:20 NIV).

They dropped everything and followed Jesus.

Can you imagine Peter's wife that evening, wondering why her husband hadn't returned to her? Can you imagine that she perhaps bumps into him later that week and asks:

"Hmmm...honey, I miss you. Are you okay?"

"Oh yes...I'm really good, sweetheart."

"Well, I miss you. What are you doing?"

"Hmmm…I'm not sure exactly, but whatever needs to be done, I am here."

"Well when can we see you again?"

"I'm not sure, baby. Jesus doesn't really have a schedule."

"Oh wow…okay then. How long will you be gone?"

"Well, again, I have no idea. I'm not sure I'm even coming back."

"What about the boat? What about our business?"

"The boat is safe, sweetheart. I just won't be doing that anymore. I am just going to be serving Jesus from now on."

Can you imagine just how irresponsible that would have sounded? Leaving your family for what? Leaving your business to become a groupie to Mary's Son, Jesus of Nazareth? And again, for how long, and to what end?

The brothers followed Jesus without knowing the plan. In fact, the plan was not for them to know. Can you imagine Jesus explaining to them how this grand adventure would end in their own executions?

I WILL BLESS YOU

Let's read Genesis 12:1-2 from the Contemporary English Version:

The Lord said to Abram: Leave your country, your family, and your relatives and go to the land that I will show you. I will bless you and make your descendants into a great nation. You will become famous and be a blessing to others.

The promise, the only promise God gave Abram was that He would bless him. Basically, "Accept My invitation to take you somewhere special. I am going to make you great! And you will have a lot of sons and daughters and out of you will be a great nation." Now remember, Abram has no children. He is around seventy years old and things don't look promising in the "baby department."

Abram does not get to say, "Okay Lord, I will follow You, but can You please first give me the coordinates?" Instead, he just follows God's instruction, and look what God did. He indeed blessed the whole world because of him. The promise did come true.

Right now, God is saying to someone, maybe you:

- "I want you to reach men for Me."
- "Let Me touch broken women through you."
- "I need to work with prison inmates."
- "Connect with the business community."
- "Will you start a homeless shelter for Me?"
- "You are to touch and impact millennials for Me."

The minister must say yes to an invitation without first understanding it.

Your mind will naturally say, "Okay, Lord, what does this mean?" or "How do I even begin, Lord?" "Where do I get the funding?" "Who is going to work with me?" These are all valid questions—but have absolutely nothing to do with His invitation. My friend, the big deal is that you do not get the answers to those questions before you say, "Yes, Lord!" You don't get the map or game plan before you step out in faith to begin.

Right now, the Holy Spirit is inviting you to step up to a magnificent dance floor of His doing. It's His music. You don't know how to do this dance—your job is to allow Him to lead this dance. "But what if I'm clumsy? Will I be disqualified?" His answer would be, "No no, you are perfect. Let us do this dance together. You serve Me, speak for Me, smile for Me, touch them for Me, feed them for Me." That is the ministry.

Is God calling you? Is He disturbing you, troubling your waters concerning His business, His Kingdom? Stand up and take the first step to walk into the fog of His invitation. He invites you to walk into what you do not know, and quite frankly, cannot know. And He expects you to respond right away and all the way because you are a *huperetes*, an under-rower.

CHAPTER 2

The Test of Conviction

Will you keep rowing in spite of the landscape?

So, Abram says yes to God's crazy invitation. Guess what happens next? He has to actually persuade his kinfolk, gather his belongings, fold up camp, and make haste to this unknown destination.

After the *Test of Faith* comes the *Test of Conviction*. This test's objective is to press you to clearly answer this question: Are you sure you want to do this?

THE PLOUGH

Jesus is famous. Multitudes want to hang out with Him and see Him touch, heal, free people from demonic oppression, etc. He is the greatest show in town. Quite frankly, it's pretty cool to be around Him.

> *On their way, someone came up to Jesus and said, "I want to follow you wherever you go"* (Luke 9:57 TPT).

This guy wants to be a groupie—a fan! He basically says to Jesus, "This is cool. I'm going to come hang out with You everywhere You go. I am in!"

Jesus replies:

> *Yes, but remember this: even animals in the field have holes in the ground to sleep in and birds have their nests, but the Son of Man has no place here to lay down his head* (Luke 9:58 TPT).

Basically Jesus says, "Okay I hear you. Great that you want to come hang out with Me, but I gotta warn you, this gig is not predictable. We don't have hotel reservations. We crash all over the countryside."

A famous prosperity preacher once said to me, "Dennis, Jesus had a treasurer, so He was rich. Also keep in mind that only rich people could afford seamless robes. And because He was rich, you and I should be rich too, brother!" Absolute rubbish! Jesus' own words tell us, "People have places to sleep. I don't." In fact, in the Message Bible translation Jesus asks the man, *"Are you ready to rough it? We're not staying in the best inns, you know."*

Serving Jesus is uncomfortable.

Well, before the guy responds, *"Jesus then turned to another and said, 'Come be my disciple'"* (Luke 9:59 TPT).

Wow, this guy is being invited to the table. Could he have been the thirteenth disciple? We'll never know. At any rate, the fellow responds, *"Lord, let me first go and bury my father"* (Luke 9:59 NKJV).

The Passion Translation puts it this way:

Someday I will, Lord, but allow me first to fulfill my duty as a good son and wait until my father passes away.

Now to the Western mind, a burial ceremony is an afternoon affair. Some readers might think that he is asking for a few hours to clear this unpleasant business. Okay, the man's response is reasonable. His dad just died. Surely Jesus understands that. Not so…

In this culture, the first son was obligated to perform the funeral rites, which lasted up to one year after the burial of his father's bones. So the man was not just saying, "Can I come back tomorrow," but rather, "Give me a few months to check back in with You, Jesus."

Jesus told him, "Don't wait for your father's burial. Let those who are already dead wait for death. But as for you, go and proclaim everywhere that God's kingdom has arrived" (Luke 9:60 TPT).

Basically, Jesus is saying, "Buddy, I am calling you to something greater than anything else." And I bet you Jesus' response draws gasps of unbelief. They must have thought, *Huh, c'mon Jesus, that is so harsh. Surely You know this is our tradition!*

That reminds me of something a minister told me: "Dr. Dennis, I am ready to go, but I just need to make sure my family is provided for before I get into the ministry." That guy will probably never step out. Is ministry intense? Absolutely!

Serving Jesus is inconvenient.

Well, just then another man says:

Lord, I want to follow you too. But first let me go home and say good-bye to my entire family (Luke 9:61 TPT).

In other words, "Okay I get it that this is not convenient, and it cannot be deferred, but I need a few hours to close things out. Right now is not really convenient for me, Jesus. I just need to put my ducks in a row."

A lot of people say, "Obviously God is calling me, I just need to make sure."

Jesus' response:

No man, having put his hand to the plough, and looking back, is fit for the kingdom of God (Luke 9:62).

Here is the picture for you: You say to the Lord, "Sign me up, Lord. I want to work!" So He assigns you a patch of farmland to work. You are given a plough or plow, a yoke, and oxen. Everything is ready. You get down to the starting line to plough and then suddenly, your eyes are elsewhere. As the oxen begin to move forward, you are looking backward. Do you think you will be able to plough straight or plough at all?

To recap, we see three people with different encounters with Jesus:

Guy #1: "I really want to follow You, but I would like to know what's next before I commit."

Jesus' response: "Sorry buddy, this journey is not predictable."

Guy #2: "I am willing go, but can I take a raincheck?"

Jesus' response: "I offer no exceptions. It's now or never!"

Guy #3: "I'm in, but need to first get my ducks in a row."

Jesus' response: "You are either in or out!"

Serving Jesus is radical.

CONVICTION

…Thou art my beloved Son; in thee I am well pleased (Luke 3:22).

Many ears would have heard those mind-blowing words—God's proclamation concerning His Son. I can imagine someone wondering, *Wait…you mean Jesus is not Mary and Joseph's son?* It must have been shocking to say the least. Remember, no one really knew about the visitation. Mary herself was tightlipped about His true identity. Can you imagine telling the Jews that Yahweh had impregnated you and that ordinary looking young man, your first-born, was God's offspring? Ridiculous, scandalous, but definitely blasphemous…and therefore extremely dangerous! No wonder Luke writes, *"Mary kept all these things in her heart and thought about them often"* (Luke 2:19 NLT).

So you would think that with such an endorsement, Jesus would march right up to Rome and declare His dominion, right? On the contrary, the Bible says that after His baptism:

Jesus was led by the Spirit into the wilderness to be tempted by the devil (Matthew 4:1 NKJV).

A keen examination of Satan's temptations in the wilderness clearly reveals a framework for the *Test of Conviction*. The questions for us posed by this test are similar to what Jesus faced: "Are you sure you are a child of God? Are you sure you want to go through with this?"

It's been five years ago when James married Sarah, his high school sweetheart. Lately though, their bond has been tested. After their second baby was born, she plummeted into postpartum depression. She gained 60 pounds and is indifferent about her appearance. She refuses to leave the house, so she doesn't attend church services anymore. Problem is, she is the pastor's wife.

Their young church begins to hurt from the turmoil.

Meanwhile, Tiffany, the children's minister has her eyes on Pastor James. She has always been attracted to him. James can't ignore her radiant smile, manicured nails, intoxicating perfume, and quick wit. She loves the ministry and will do anything he asks of her. Suddenly James faces the *Test of Conviction*. Will he give in to Tiffany's charm, or love his broken wife back to health?

See, their wedding day was just a ceremony of intensions. The wedding vows were an expression of his plan to permanently hook up with Sarah, merge their finances, raise a family, and do life together. Until he passes this *Test of Conviction*, James merely *intended* to be married to Sarah.

Tom quits his seven-figure executive job and plans to relocate his family to Haiti. Just before he is to leave, his wife insists on a full health checkup. "There is a small benign tumor on your lungs," Doctor Jacobs says. "You are going to Haiti, I hear. Although the chances of this thing growing are slim to none, I would strongly advise against a move like that. You never know what could happen over there." Tom is facing a *Test of Conviction*.

He must pass it or face the possibility of never really getting into full-time missions.

"Daughter, I want you to give $200 to the Smiths every month," instructs the Lord. Dora is excited. She is happy to bless this struggling family. She immediately writes the first check. Two months later, she learns of a merger that threatens her position. "Ugh, I don't think it's wise to give that much," she reasons, "especially since I might lose my job. I should save that money for my family." Dora is facing a *Test of Conviction*.

My friend Apostle Grace Lubega recently shared this troubling story with me. A famous international speaker was scheduled to visit Uganda a couple of years back. Believers across the city were super excited, in anticipation of a mighty visitation of the Holy Spirit, particularly because the country was reeling from a cholera outbreak. Suddenly, the preacher cancels the visit, reason being he didn't want to risk exposure to the deadly disease. Everyone was shocked and frankly disheartened. They couldn't wrap their minds around the thought – a man of God afraid of catching an illness? To make matters worse, a famous reggae superstar who was booked to tour the country at the same time decides to boldly show up. Grace told me, "I wept when I saw the images; 10,000 fans screaming at the top of their lungs while we had to cancel our event. Dennis, to us, it seemed as though this heathen had greater faith than the man of God."

Paul writes:

> *But for now, I feel a stirring in my heart to send Epaph-roditus back to you immediately. He's a friend to me and a wonderful brother and fellow soldier who has worked with me as we serve as ministers of the gospel. And you sent him as your apostle to minister to me in my need.*

But now he is grieved to know that you found out he had been sick, so he longs to return and comfort you in this. It's true he almost died, but God showed him mercy and healed him. And I'm so thankful to God for his healing, as I was spared from having the sorrow of losing him on top of all my other troubles! So you can see why I'm delighted to send him to you now. I know that you're anxious to see him and rejoice in his healing, and it encourages me to know how happy you'll be to have him back. So warmly welcome him home in the Lord, with joyous love, and esteem him highly, for people like him deserve it. Because of me, he put his life on the line, despising the danger, so that he could provide for me with what you couldn't, since you were so far away. And he did it all because of his ministry for Christ (Philippians 2:25-30 TPT).

There is so much locked up in Paul's earned entreaty. He is clearly bragging on a truly special man. Epaphroditus was very sick when the brethren sent him to encourage Paul. He went nonetheless but without saying a word about his condition. It would seem that he became deathly ill in the commission of his assignment, except for God's healing grace. In other words, faced with the test of conviction, Epaphroditus pressed on in spite of his poor health. Rare these days.

It is 1992. We've just won the Best New Artists Award at Britain's DMI Awards, Europe's then equivalent to America's Dove Awards. After three years of immense toil, it seems like we have broken through. The media had dubbed us "Britain's answer to America's Boyz 2 Men!" We are booked every week around Europe. Suddenly the Lord says to us, "I want you to move to America." What? Now? Why would we leave England now? We wrestled with this test even as confirmation after confirmation came through.

Yes, indeed this was the Lord. So we did the "Abraham-thing," selling everything to relocate to America.

One of the band members is hesitant. His family insists that he finish school first. I remember it like it was yesterday. "Guys, I cannot go. My family expects me to finish school." We pleaded with him to reconsider. We were a tight band of brothers. We dreamed together, wrote together, and ate together in our modest London house. Without him, everything would change—harmony structures, stage presence, even repertoire. Suddenly we faced a *Test of Conviction*. To give it up, stay with our friend, get "real" jobs and play it safe, or jump out of the boat and do crazy! We had to pass it. We bid our friend farewell, left London, then onward to America where the group exploded to global iconic status, literally touching millions around the world with our music.

Here is a phrase I have heard 10,000 times: "I want to submit under you, Dr. Dennis. Please correct me and guide me." I used to be flattered when someone honored me like that. Not anymore. I came to realize that such a bold declaration is merely an intention. When I corrected them or attempted to guide them, then I knew if they were really ready for the accountability that the coaching relationship required.

Untested commitments are mere intentions.

Submission doesn't come alive until those who advise tell us to go left when we think we should go right, or sit still when we think we must run. I have asked some eager sons, "Are you sure you want to call me spiritual father? Of course, I will be your biggest cheerleader, but as a spiritual father, don't expect me to constantly affirm you or celebrate you when you are neglecting your family, for example." Many don't ask me again. They drift away, failing the *Test of Conviction*. Remember, untested relationships are just acquaintances.

FINISHERS

Paul writes:

> *Moreover it is required in stewards, that one be found faithful* (1 Corinthians 4:2 NKJV).

The Greek word for faithful in that verse is *pistos*, which means trustworthy.

Jesus is performing miracles, healing every manner of illness, and feeding thousands. The fame of His marvelous works swells, so much so that they want to crown Him king. Then Jesus says:

> *Truly, truly, I say to you, unless you eat the flesh of the Son of Man and drink His blood, you have no life in yourselves. He who eats My flesh and drinks My blood has eternal life, and I will raise him up on the last day. For My flesh is true food, and My blood is true drink* (John 6:53-55 New American Standard Bible).

Wow…campaign over! Jesus wants us to eat His flesh? Jesus is the *bread of life* (John 6:35). Eating Him means believing in Him, but they don't know that. The crowd takes offense. Many fall away.

So He turns to His inner circle and asks them if they are leaving as well.

Simon Peter answered him, "Lord, to whom shall we go? You have the words of eternal life. We have believed and have come to know that You are the Holy One of God" (John 6:68-69 New American Standard Bible).

In other words, Peter says, "Nope, we are ready to pass this *Test of Conviction*. We are not leaving because You say something that we do not like or understand."

Are you really a minister, or is ministry simply showmanship to you? Are you going to follow Jesus, even when the cost becomes bigger than you thought—like when you realize that you'll probably lose your friends, job, popularity, and family? When you say, "Jesus, please come into my life. I am going to live for You," it is a great day that memorializes your intention to live for Christ. But it is not real until you faithfully choose Christ and really prove your commitment to Him.

Have you ever hung out at the starting line of a major marathon? It's amazing. Everybody has the latest gear, they all look great, they are bouncing around, stretching, intimidating each other with their designer head caps, and are all ready to run the punishing twenty-seven-mile marathon.

Now jump into your car and drive to the finish line and look at them. First of all, only a handful get that far—and nobody looks good at the finish line. They are all sweaty, they can barely breathe. But they are finishers.

Many people have said to me, "The Lord has told me to travel with you, and to serve your ministry." I say, "Great!" Some even pass the *Test of Faith*. They actually adjust their lifestyles and actively put money aside to participate in their first mission trip. Big step, right? But I typically wait for the second trip, which is predictably harder. Why? The *Test of Conviction*. A few months down the road, and they are gone. Great starters…poor finishers.

If you vowed to serve Jesus, then just do it! If you are a wife, be a wife! If husband, be one! If you are a friend, come on, be a friend! Over the years I have seen people pay the price for being my friend. They have been attacked and some have had to fight for me. Someone said to me, "Yeah, I heard somebody lambasting you the other day. He was defaming your character. I chose to just stay out of it."

I was upset. "You actually heard someone spreading lies about me and you said nothing?" My true friends will fight for me even before they hear the full story.

If thou faint in the day of adversity, thy strength is small (Proverbs 24:10).

That means friend, there is going to come a day of adversity. It brings with it this *Test of Conviction.* If you fail during that time, your strength is small. Resolve to serve God and realize that He won't show you any part of the map until after you say yes. He will not say:

"Okay now, your job is going to be phased out, so you are about to be laid off. I have another job for you, but it will not come for about nine months, during which time you are going to run out of savings. I need to teach you how to trust Me, so I will frustrate your plan B. I have sent you teachers to teach you. I have sent you books to read. I have sent you clips to view, but you are not getting it. Now we are going to do it the old fashioned way: I am going to suspend you, dangle you, and you will say, 'God, my life is in Your hands,' and you will sing out, 'Lord, my life is in Your hands.'

Then, I shall rescue you. And I shall put you up on a high place. Yeah, that is what I am going to do."

> *We can't walk by faith until we don't know the plan.*

Sounds great to know ahead of time, right? Fact is, if God showed you the map, you would tinker with it. Besides, knowing what's ahead means that you'd be walking by hope, not faith. After you've said yes to His wild invitation to *hupereteo*, stand firm. Do not falter. Do not look back. Do not turn back. Pass the *Test of Conviction*. You are a *huperetes*…bound to a sacred duty! Be comforted by Paul's timeless words:

> *…Then after the battle you will still be standing firm* (Ephesians 6:13 NLT).

CHAPTER 3

The Test of Isolation

Will you keep rowing after everyone else goes home?

Will you serve Jesus, even after everyone else has quit? Can you walk the journey without company? What do you do when God calls you into enclosures of separation? Talk to any serious minister or any dedicated servant of God, and they will tell you of that dreadful season when they took their *Test of Isolation*.

JACOB

Jacob is a miracle baby born to sixty-year-old Isaac and Rebekah. As he develops, Jacob becomes a mama's boy. While his brother is out in the wild doing "manly" things, Jacob prefers to hang around the house with his mother. Jacob tricks his brother Esau to obtain the blessing of the firstborn, giving him superiority and the coveted double portion of his wealthy dad's inheritance. Genesis 27:41 says, *"Esau hated Jacob…"*

Thus begins Jacob's season of running, with his mama of course, first to Syria. He ends up laboring for twenty years for Laban. From there, he fled to Canaan with his wives and kids—a self-inflicted, miserable existence far removed from the bliss of his father's house. Deep inside Jacob knows he must do something to change the trajectory of his life, beginning with reconciling with his deeply offended brother, Esau. The pressure leads him to a propitious kairos moment.

Pressure is a well-trodden meeting point with Divinity.

During the night Jacob got up and took his two wives, his two servant wives, and his eleven sons and crossed the Jabbok River with them. After taking them to the other side, he sent over all his possessions. This left Jacob all alone in the camp... (Genesis 32:22-24 NLT).

Nighttime often brings danger, darkness, cold, uncertainty, inconvenience, and discomfort. It is at "night" when God calls us to isolation. In other words, it is during seasons of:

- *Transitions* such as menopause, mid-life crisis, retirement, etc.

- *Intrusions* such as the death of a loved one, illness, accidents, bankruptcy, divorce, etc.

- *Disenchantment* such as burnout, spousal affairs, relentless "there-has-to-be-more-to-life-than-this" rumblings, etc.

- *Suffocation* such as when: church becomes stifling; songs don't touch you anymore; reading the Bible is boring; things that used to matter no longer do; things that never mattered become paramount; and it feels like your life has curled up into a frightening question mark.

If you are there right now, it's time to pull up a chair. You are about to take the *Test of Isolation.*

When the man saw that he would not win the match, he touched Jacob's hip and wrenched it out of its socket (Genesis 32:25 NLT).

Do we honestly think that God was beaten by Jacob? Of course not. God simply puts His finger on the seat of his strength to cause him to quit. One translation says that Jacob's sinew shrunk. That would have produced excruciating pain. Consequently, Jacob collapses in the arms of the Lord, a picture of complete reliance. The objective of the all-night fight is to take Jacob to the limit of his desperation. Why? Here is a thought worth noting. God must confound, astonish, and flabbergast Jacob. Feathers must be ruffled, because it is only then that a different man can emerge, or the entire wrestling match is a wasted experience. Notice that only when the fighting stops does real transformation begin.

You see, Jacob wants more, so he pleads: *"I will not let you go unless you bless me"* (Genesis 32:26 NLT).

"'What is your name?' the man asked. He replied, 'Jacob'" (Genesis 32:27 NLT), which by the way means deceiver or supplanter. The encounter has changed him. His name must also change.

*"Your name will no longer be Jacob," the man told him.
"From now on you will be called Israel, because you have
fought with God and with men and have won"* (Genesis
32:28 NLT).

Jacob is no doubt relieved, but he has a question, *"Please tell me
your name"* (Genesis 32:29 NLT).

In other words, I thought I knew You. I thought I knew who I
was fighting. I was sorely mistaken. You are way bigger, stronger,
more majestic! The Lord's response is really curious, *"Why do you
want to know my name?"*

In that culture, names spoke of identity. God was basically
saying, "No, you don't need to figure Me out. I am not one thing,
Israel. You cannot figure Me out...but in your searching, you
have found *you*." In fact, Jacob now Israel doesn't get an answer
but instead receives a mega, transgenerational blessing right there
at Peniel.

Your true identity does not come from a denomination, label,
or a belief system, but from Peniel. Your journey must bring you
to this place where God uncurls your grip, finger by finger, and
invites you to dismantle old masks and unfold a deeper more
authentic *you*.

I suggest an overnight stay at Peniel. Have the courage, I pray,
to accept the invitation to be alone, to be separated.

The minister must break the
addiction to cheerleaders.

JOHN THE BAPTIST

For he shall be great in the sight of the Lord, and shall drink neither wine nor strong drink; and he shall be filled with the Holy Ghost, even from his mother's womb. And many of the children of Israel shall he turn to the Lord their God. And he shall go before him in the spirit and power of Elias, to turn the hearts of the fathers to the children, and the disobedient to the wisdom of the just; to make ready a people prepared for the Lord (Luke 1:15-17).

This Scripture passage describes John the Baptist. He is a man who was filled with the Holy Spirit even before his birth. His was a prophetic birth—a boy-child fully consecrated to the Lord. John grew up to be someone who was kind of…out there. He wore strange clothing made of camel hair and had an odd diet consisting of honey and locusts. But boy was he a phenomenon! His fame reached throughout Judea and throngs of people trekked to the wilderness to hear his powerful message: REPENT AND BE BAPTIZED!

Not long after John explained to his massive crowds that he was not the promised Messiah, he sees his cousin Jesus at the front of the baptism line. Right there, he speaks by the Spirit of God:

Behold! The Lamb of God who takes away the sin of the world! (John 1:29 NKJV)

In other words, "Here He is! This is who I have prepared the way for." As John baptizes Jesus, God Himself speaks audibly:

You are My beloved Son; in You I am well pleased (Luke 3:22 NKJV).

In just a few months, Jesus' fame has ballooned! He is working miracles, healing the sick, casting out demons, cleansing lepers, multiplying food...oh, and He is raising the dead too!

As a result, John's crowds began to dwindle. And why wouldn't they? He outright told them that Jesus was greater than him and, evidenced by the miracles, there was no better place to be than attending a Jesus meeting. John professes:

> *"...Therefore, I am filled with joy at his success. He must become greater and greater, and I must become less and less"* (John 3:29-30 NLT).

John spoke out against Herod and was jailed for it. Suddenly, things didn't look great for him! As John sat in prison with his life hanging in the balance, he probably wondered, *Is this it? All my life has been about these short six months? Is God done with me? What if I missed it?* While he sat on death row, John hears of the wonders of Jesus—the miracles and tremendous healings.

He pondered his sorry estate.

As the days rolled on, John decided to send his disciples to ask Jesus directly, *"Are you the one who is to come, or should we expect someone else?"* (Matthew 11:2-3 NIV).

John was in essence saying, "Because my personal life is falling apart; because I can't understand what Jesus is really up to, I am having second thoughts about Jesus' identity. I am not so sure any more about my prophetic declaration. This Jesus must not be the one." What? Wait a minute. Did John just ask that? The man who was filled with the Holy Spirit, even before his birth? He was the harbinger of Christ, the guy who basically introduces Jesus to the Jews. Besides…did he not actually hear God's audible voice affirming Jesus?

Clearly, things hadn't turned out like John thought. Jesus was not playing to John's script. And that, my friend, was John's problem. Right there in Herod's holding cell, John faced a brutal *Test of Isolation*.

If you have been there, like I have been many times, you know exactly what John was feeling. When crisis isolates us, we naturally feel as though God must not be with us, because we believe that God is supposed to protect us, save us, cover us, and prosper us.

Jesus did not answer John's disciples question. Instead, Jesus said:

Go back and report to John what you hear and see: The blind receive sight, the lame walk, those who have leprosy are cleansed, the deaf hear, the dead are raised, and the good news is proclaimed to the poor (Matthew 11:4-5 NIV).

Jesus didn't offer verbal proof of His authenticity. Here is how I read this: "Tell John what you're seeing Me do. Tell John that he must have faith in God even though he doesn't see His hand right now. He has to trust in God even though he is not experiencing His blessings. Instead of nursing his broken soul, My beloved cousin John must focus on My work. He must look at what I am doing, not what I am not doing."

We don't how John responded to Jesus' response. But Jesus cautions:

Blessed is anyone who does not stumble on account of me (Matthew 11:6 NIV).

Authentic faith sees the unseen,
touches the intangible.

ALONE

As a new believer, I always had close friends running with me—David, Michael, Robert, Fred. You'd never find me alone. We would pray together, witness together, and suffer together. In fact, my friends always ended up moving in with my family. We were not rich by any means. In fact, they just crashed in the front room of our tiny two-bedroom flat along with the nine of us. I celebrate my mother for allowing this company. Without these guys, I would not be here. It was great to have someone to pray with in the wee hours of the morning; to cut covenants before the Lord with; to do long fasts with or to stay on my knees for hours and hours with.

But I remember, in the midst of all of that camaraderie, when the Lord started to invite me to places of isolation, saying, "Dennis, I want you to wake up at 2 a.m." Immediately, I'd tell my buddy what the Lord said. I vividly remember the Lord correcting me, "No, no, no, YOU wake up at 2 a.m.!"

I remember thinking, *Wait, Lord, what is Fred going to think if he hears me praying alone?*

One day, the Spirit of the Lord instructed me, "I want you to get off your bed and to sleep on a mat. You will do this until I instruct you otherwise!" Again, I thought about my friend. We had done so much together. He will be thrilled to hear what the Lord wants us to do. Like Abram, I took Lot with me. I remember feeling troubled.

It took a while for the Lord to persuade me that He was calling me, isolating me for an assignment that required greater consecration and sacrifice.

A few years later, we formed a special prophetic intercessory group called Ephesus. About thirty young men pledged to live a dedicated, on-fire life for God. We had all-night prayer meetings. We encountered visitations of angels and saw incredible miracles, signs, wonders that I have not seen since. We were radical. I remember spending entire days in unceasing prayer in the Spirit. I mean twelve hours of what we called stammering lips. I still remember my perplexity when the Lord asked me to stop going to Ephesus. "What? Lord, Ephesus is it! Why would You want me to leave?" He was silent. I obeyed...

For the next seventeen years, my friends and I literally lived together as we served in a global music ministry called Limit X. We toured the nations and built a legacy in the music industry that is still unmatched in Africa's history. But I still remember that cold Chicago day when the Lord said, "It is time to put the music away!" I thought it was the devil. Granted we had endured some bumps, but I really thought we could keep our ministry going well into our 80s.

Just like that, I was alone and again facing the *Test of Isolation*. The Spirit of the Lord was asking, "Dennis, will you do it alone?"

Jesus says:

> *Think not that I am come to send peace on earth: I came not to send peace, but a sword. For I am come to set a man at variance against his father, and the daughter against her mother, and the daughter in law against her mother in law* (Matthew 10:34-35).

What? Jesus divides families? Yep…

"Ingrid, you feel alone sometimes, don't you?" I asked my wife one day.

"Yes I do. I am lonely a lot." I felt terrible. I very much wanted to rescue her. "Sometimes I just miss intelligent, adult conversations," she said. Ingrid does not have a lot of friends visiting these days. Everyone is doing their own lives. They are too busy to look in on her.

Ingrid has had to pay this price by herself. When we married, she was pulled away from her close-knit Romanian culture. I was a full-time recording artist at the time. We immediately hit the road, then came the scrutiny and criticism. Prior to our engagement, some of our mentors had cautioned, "God has a future for you, but watch out for those women. They will bring doom to the ministry."

Ingrid was critically scrutinized by family, friends, mentors, and the media. "Does she pray long enough?" "Is she fasting for the ministry like a good wife should?" "She should be selling your product instead of hanging out backstage." They gave her all kinds of grief. It was very difficult for her. I could not help her. And as much as I cried with her, she was being called into the ministry. Life was asking this question: "Are you going to serve and walk with this man, even though he has two guys tied to him at the hip?" Since then, she is has become familiar with the *Test of Isolation*.

Decline the invitation to isolation,
and you cannot become.

DE-CLUSTER

Everybody I respect has had this inconvenient invitation to be separate. Simply put, you will never walk into your assignment unless you accept the invitation to disconnect and fall on your face before your God alone. It is at the place of isolation where you get to hear God for yourself. There is where you drop the clichés and discover what sanctification, prayer, and intimacy really means. It is there that you break the codependency on collectivism. You realize that perhaps you don't really need to fly out of state to attend another conference, buy the latest best-selling book, or subscribe to the hottest Christian podcast.

The *Test of Isolation* forces you to answer these questions:

1. Do I really believe it?

2. Do I believe it even after the lights are out?

3. Do I believe it when I am down and out?

4. Do I really believe it even when my circle doesn't?

5. Can I shout as loud, dance as hard, pray as long, love as passionately…ALONE?

I am going to say something that may trouble you, but please allow it to sit with you. There is no such a thing as a dual calling. I hear guys say, "Yeah the Lord definitely wants me to launch a ministry, but my wife doesn't like it, so I guess I really can't. My wife and I have got to be in agreement for us to do anything." Certainly this sounds caring, but I am sorry it is not biblical. "But Dr. Dennis, my most important ministry is my family." Again, not biblical either. Doing family is not a ministry. It's a duty born out of a sense of obligation and commitment.

You are blessed to obey God's call on your life by yourself. I have seen the enemy stop people from obeying God because of this philosophy. I have heard, "She is okay when I go golfing with the guys, but when I want to go to a men's retreat, she doesn't feel I should. I guess I'll wait until we are in agreement." And, "My husband is happy to go shopping, but can't stand the women's Bible study. He thinks it's a waste of time. I guess I can't serve God that way." Now am I advising couples to just go renegade and do whatever? Of course not.

Someone may say, "But my whole church is called." Yes, God can place a mandate on a leader or team for a region; but guess what, He still calls everybody to come along individually. My experience leading ministry groups on six continents for four decades has taught me that what may feel like a group calling never is. That is why every authentic minister must get to the place where they answer the call of God by themselves.

Consider what our Beloved Lord Jesus says:

Behold, the hour cometh, yea, is now come, that ye shall be scattered, every man to his own, and shall leave me alone: and yet I am not alone, because the Father is with me (John 16:32).

"But I need company," you might protest. "I don't want to be an isolationist."

C.S. Lewis wrote in his essay "The Inner Ring":

I believe…one of the most dominant elements is the desire to be inside the local Ring and the terror of being left outside. …Of all the passions, the passion for the Inner Ring is most skillful in making a man who is not yet a very bad man do very bad things. …As long as you're governed by that desire [to be in the Inner Ring] you will never get what you want. You are trying to peel an onion: if you succeed, there will be nothing left. Until you conquer the fear of being an outsider, an outsider you will remain. …But if all you want is to be in the know, your pleasure will be short lived. The circle cannot have from within the charm it had from outside. By the very fact of admitting you it has lost its magic. Once the first novelty is worn off, the members of this circle will be no more interesting than your old friends. Why should they be? …You merely wanted to be "in." And that is a pleasure that cannot last.[1]

Basically, we always long to be what we are not. You wish you were the pastor or that you were part of that group. You wish you were a business leader, a well-known speaker, or whatever ring you admire. Out there, there is a ring that seems glittery and screams an invite to you. But what C.S. Lewis is saying is that once you actually get admitted to that ring, it loses its luster because now you are part of it. Besides, how could it be as attractive when you are in it? You really wish you could belong to the millionaire's club until you become one. You wish you were part of the married group until you get married. Simply put, the ring is overrated.

Here is what I want to say as we bring this chapter to a close. Can we determine that when God decides to pull us out of a ring and isolate and disconnect us, we will not fight Him?

Learn to embrace the stillness that births destiny.

Be still and know that I am God... (Psalm 46:10).

Stillness means waiting. Noah waits for the waters; Sarah waits for her Isaac; Joseph waits for his promise; Moses waits for the deliverance of his people; Daniel waits through the night; Jonah waits in a fish. Contrary to what our quick-aholic culture believes, real transformation is never instant and is not a mass experience.

I'll close with my favorite verse from God's Word:

> *But they that wait upon the Lord shall renew their strength; they shall mount up with wings as eagles; they shall run, and not be weary; and they shall walk, and not faint* (Isaiah 40:31).

Endnote

1. C.S. Lewis (1898-1963), *The Inner Ring* essay delivered at the Memorial Lecture at King's College, University of London, 1944; https://www.lewissociety.org/innerring/; accessed February 15, 2020.

CHAPTER 4

The Test of Servanthood

Will you keep rowing even when no one really sees you?

So then you must perceive us—not as leaders of factions, but as servants of the Anointed One, those who have been entrusted with God's mysteries (1 Corinthians 4:1 TPT).

What a powerful verse! We are not leaders, but servants charged with the mammoth responsibility of stewarding God's mysteries.

Allow me to employ a simplified, less theological interpretation of the word "mysteries."

We have no clue how a sinner gets saved, how an addiction is shattered, how a curse is broken, or how a limb is healed. We do not get to understand how God does His work among us, do we? I have often said at the beginning of our events, "Guys, I am not smart enough, eloquent enough, or brilliant enough to persuade you concerning the condition of your soul." Indeed, I could intellectually make a case for Jesus, for salvation and missions, but only the Holy Spirit can draw men and women to Himself. Only He removes the veil of blindness so they can see His glorious light.

Friend, we are merely servants. This Good News is not ours. It is too complex, too magnificent, too awesome, too glorious, too incredible for us fathom, to unpack, or to pick at. We are but mere stewards.

THE LITMUS TEST

Mary tearfully announces, "Pastor Tom, you have really changed my life!"

Big words, right? Naturally humbling and clearly undeserved. You know full well, you did nothing to put her marriage back in order or get her philandering, gambling husband to settle down and be the godly leader he is now. But when pastors and ministry leaders hear that over and over for decades, it starts to get to them, to us. Many of us begin to think that we are amazing. We forget that we are merely servants, completely incapable of washing sins away, healing broken hearts, or mending fractured bonds. We are stewards entrusted with God's mysteries.

Jesus is the big deal, not me.

I was invited as a keynote speaker at a large church in Texas one summer. My team inconspicuously dropped me off at the front door so I could enter the auditorium with everybody else. I was dressed plainly, no suit, nothing flashy.

"Welcome, sir," the greeter said. "We think you are special. I want to encourage you that Jesus loves you. Whenever you feel discouraged, take this card out and read it. It'll help you." I was tempted to introduce myself, "I am Dr. Dennis, the guest speaker tonight." But suddenly, I felt so "normal." And indeed, I was not anything special. I was but a servant.

Just then the executive pastor shouted from across the hall, "Oh my gosh, Christina, that's our guest, Dr. Dennis. We're so sorry. Pastor is waiting for you in the back office." Christina, the gracious greeter, was almost embarrassed, but I said, "Thank you, Christina, I will keep this card. You have ministered to me."

Back to that verse at the beginning of the chapter: *"So then you must perceive us—not as leaders of factions, but as servants of the Anointed One, those who have been entrusted with God's mysteries"* (1 Corinthians 4:1 TPT).

Paul instructs me not to perceive myself as a leader of a "faction," namely Eagle's Wings International or THE 300, but a servant. Yes, we might serve as senior pastors, team leaders, bishops, apostles, and overseers, but we are servants first. The big question is how do we respond when others treat us as regular people, much less servants?

In fact, will you take a moment and ponder this haunting question: Can you act like a servant, when you are treated like one? Do you want to know how you know if you are really a servant? Watch how you respond when someone spits on you or overlooks you and treats you badly. Does it irk you that they don't recognize you or can't tell who you are?

THE WAY TO THE TOP

Then they came to Capernaum. And as soon as Jesus was inside the house, he asked his disciples, "What were you arguing about on the way here?" No one said a word, because they had been arguing about which one of them was the greatest (Mark 9:33-34 TPT).

Let that scene sink in for a moment!

Jesus is the talk of the town, and the entire region in fact. The Man who touches people and they are healed; the Man who makes food out of nothing; the Man who raises the dead and cleanses lepers. He is the brilliant Man who can out argue all of the smartest scholars. Consequently, His crew is envied. Being a member of Jesus' entourage was a most coveted position.

So His guys are thinking, *This is huge. There are members of the Sanhedrin privately coming to see Jesus, even Roman soldiers are talking about Him. Pretty soon, Caesar will summon Him. Nothing can possibly stop His assent!* Remember, they believed Jesus to be the Messiah who would restore Israel. There is no doubt they must have fantasized about marching on Rome and sitting next to Jesus as He assumes power from Israel's oppressors.

They are not selfish. They are not egoists. They are human. Humans want to ascend. We like to let people know who we are; to show we are better, greater, more eloquent, more skilled, more productive. Do that effectively, and we will ascend.

Jesus discerns their ponderings and introduces a profound truth: *"If anyone wants to be first, he must be content to be last and become a servant to all"* (Mark 9:35 TPT).

In other words, "In My government, the way to the top is the bottom." Notice that He did not say that it is wrong to be want to be first. There is false piety that exists in some ministries. "No, no, no, I do not want to lead. I will just stay in the back." Jesus did not chide them for wanting to be leaders. He just provided a mind-blowingly counterintuitive path to the top. Wanna be first? Contend to be last!

Here is a powerful statement: In the Kingdom of God, the way to the top is the bottom. I often say to apprentices and prospective church leaders, "If you want the pulpit, the microphone, or the stage, then look for the rag, the mop, and the broom. Show me your calloused hands. That is your pathway. That is how you become a leader."

We descend to the top.

In secular organizations, bosses like to stay at the top with everybody else beneath them. That is the common leadership pyramid. Well, Jesus inverts it. The leader is placed at the bottom with everyone else on top.

There is a difference between volunteerism and servanthood. A volunteer will say, "I want to serve, but only if you can meet my conditions or terms." They might do the same things a servant does, but the heart, the attitude, is different.

"Hey John, will you go to the other door to greet today," instructs the head usher. "There is a guy I would like you to keep an eye on. He seems fidgety."

John is immediately triggered. He is offended. "But I told you I don't like working that side of the auditorium. My family sits in this section and I hear better with this ear. It's where I have served for the last sixteen years!"

Indeed, John has served faithfully over the years. It suddenly seems like he has been a blessing to the church, only as long as his serving conditions were met. He was in if the head usher met his preconditions for service. Bluntly put, John is a volunteer, not a servant.

Beware of volunteerism. It is faux-servanthood. As a servant, your job is to place others' needs ahead of yours. You are not the main show. Often times you will be treated as a second-class citizen.

"But this is my seat!"

"You know I'm not a morning person."

"Staying thirty minutes longer isn't going to work for me!"

"This is my section!"

"I told you I don't do kids!"

Just because they arrive early to set up the chairs does not mean that they are servants. Just because they project a can-do spirit doesn't mean that they are ready to be walked over. Intriguingly, many volunteers feel entitled to a certain kind of treatment. In fact, the hallmark of a volunteer is a pervasive sense of entitlement.

A true servant has no rights.

ENTITLEMENT

I share friendships with people of high esteem—superstars, tycoons, celebrities, and royalty. These folks normally have stewards around them, attending to their needs. The constant attention inevitably creates entitlement. They struggle with otherwise normal curveballs that life throws at every one of us. They don't understand why things don't go their way. "Why do I need to apologize for my harsh tone?" "Why should I care if everyone has been waiting for me for hours?" They are special, right? Sadly, I see some of this same attitude in ministry.

God's servants have always had to deal with the tension between how we want to be treated and how we are really treated. The determinant is what I call a person's entitlement quotient.

Is the servant of the Lord entitled to honor, respect, or decorum? Do we get to throw tantrums when we are not respected as we wish? Should we even assert our authority at all?

"You never call him Dennis!" a pastor yelled. "He is Dr. Dennis to you." One of my team members had addressed me by my first name to the offense of my host. Now as much as I understand honor and respect for those over us as it says in Romans 13:7 (NKJV), *"Render therefore to all their due...honor to whom honor,"* there is something wrong with insisting that someone be addressed by their title or they feel disrespected. I am not owed any earthly respect. I have no such rights. If I become undone because I was not addressed correctly, then I have forgotten that I am a *huperetes...* just an under-rower, a mere servant.

The *Test of Servanthood*—fail it enough, and you cannot move to your next station. Jesus said:

He that is faithful in that which is least is faithful also in much... (Luke 16:10).

In other words, "Hey, I want to give you more, but you have got to show that you can steward the little. Tend to small before you qualify to look after big!"

How do I learn to bend my knee before men? Easy—if you know that you are called to steward mysteries, then you know that you have no right of ownership over anything. Knowing this deep inside enables you to act like it. When they say, "Wow, you're so anointed." Or, "I'm so glad to meet you. Your prayers saved me!" your response should be wonder, amusement, and bewilderment, not concerning your ability or ministerial proficiency but His work in you. You don't take any credit because you really know it isn't you. You are a steward!

Conversely, when they say, "We don't really like your ministry here," or, "If you weren't so direct, your ministry would be bigger," your response must reflect humility and honor. Jesus said:

God blesses you when people mock you and persecute you and lie about you and say all sorts of evil things against you because you are my followers (Matthew 5:11 NLT).

Let's read again that passage in Mark 9:35 (TPT) where Jesus says: *"If anyone wants to be first, he must be content to be last and become a servant of all."*

"Well, I have been walking with Jesus for thirty years."

"This is not my first rodeo, buddy. I was saved before you were born."

"Hey, I was here when this church opened its doors for the first time."

"Stop treating me like I just got here."

Servant of all, right?

It's easy to take it when kings, presidents, and leaders treat you like a servant. They are bigger, richer, smarter, more prominent, right? But what if people who are supposedly under you, people you perceive to be less than you, treat you like you are less than them? Do you feel a need to assert yourself, since after all, you have seniority, elevation or more experience? Jesus' prescription: Want to be first? Then want to be last. Sounds oxymoronic, doesn't it? The criteria for wanting to be first is to be happy being last.

Servanthood is born when we banish entitlement. That doesn't happen until we fully bend our knee to the lordship of Jesus Christ. If the Lord has invited you to adventure with Him, then surely He knows the way there, right?

"God, You have given me this wife, but she is always sick. I think taking up this pastorate was a mistake." "Lord, he just lost his job and can't take care of us. I'm not sure I heard You on this one."

This is where it all begins. Will you bend your knee even though you see a glaring contradiction between what you perceive should be and what really is? What do you do when it looks like your Lord gave you the wrong orders? Therein is the ultimate *Test of Servanthood*. A servant does not say, "Wait, you told me to put the towels away, why do you now want me to sweep the front room?" A true servant thinks, "Okay, I guess it's not my business. Your will, Lord, not mine!" Your prevailing attitude should always be: "Of course I will do it," "Of course I will go," "Of course I will be!"

A servant is without entitlements. A servant does not get to dictate his or her own estate. A servant obeys. A servant, *pistos*, is faithful to the household affairs—to the stewardship of the mysteries of Christ.

Here is the bottom line: When you know you are nothing, you do not get all wound up when people treat you like you are nothing.

If you know you are dirt, you don't get upset when people trample you underfoot.

FEEDBACK

A servant does not need to be told, "Well done." A hireling does. A volunteer does. Ministry is hard work. Remember, you are a *huperetes*, and to *hupereteo*, to row the ministry forward, is brutal, endless work. We get to show up early, stay longer, give more, be mistreated, overlooked, and feel downtrodden.

Everybody who has been elevated in ministry will take you back to their place of smallness and service where they were broken. They have cleaned toilets, mopped hallways, arranged chairs, or swept sidewalks. They can take you back to the place of servanthood, where they served without applause. The sad irony is that after many get the microphone, they forget those places of humbleness. They develop amnesia.

What do you do when people do not appreciate you or pat you on the back? As a *huperetes*, you must divorce yourself of feedback.

You show up. Preach. Serve. Speak. You do not need to read message boards to continue serving Jesus effectively. Why? Because you don't work for them. You are His servant. He is your Lord. You work for Jesus. Now some have used that mindset to become manipulative and controlling, but that doesn't mean that we become subservient to those we serve.

I go places because Jesus sends me. People can bless me financially me, fly me, and honor me, but I do not work for humans as a minister. So, I neither seek nor wait for their approval. When I teach or preach, I don't need them to say, "That was really good, Dr. Dennis."

When you sing, sing for Jesus. I totally understand asking your host if he or she liked a particular song or asks you to speak on a particular theme, but at the end of the day, you work for Jesus. *Huperetes*, you better not give anyone the power to approve of your service for Jesus—because you are *His* workman.

Matthew 20:1-16 outlines an interesting parable. The owner of a vineyard goes to the marketplace at the first hour of the morning to hire workers for one denarius for the day. A generous pay indeed, in fact equivalent to a Roman soldier's pay for a day. Needless to say, the workers are excited. As the day progressed, more workers were hired at the same wage; four groups in all.

When the time came for the guys to be paid, the first group of workers saw the last group being paid a denarius; although they initially were excited, they became angry even though they got exactly what they had agreed upon when they were hired.

Bottom line—it is the owner, Jesus, who has hired us who gets to decide our reward.

"Hey, I was saved thirty-seven years ago. But now this kid, who has only been saved for twelve years is running a larger church!"

"Why is she speaking on stage when I'm not? I have far more experience than she does."

I know many pastors or fathers in the faith who should be fathering right now but they are busy competing with their spiritual sons. They say things like, "You know what? I have two hundred people, and he has one thousand. I led that kid to the Lord." Well, what's it to you if the Master has decided to use the lad in that way?

We do not get to compare our ministries to anyone else's. We are servants. Papa has called upon you to serve Him, and that is all that matters. How long, how wide, how deeply He chooses to use us is entirely His prerogative. Whether He sits us down or accelerates us is His business. Our job is to say, "Yes, Master! Yes, Lord! Use me, Lord. I am Your *huperetes!*"

Let me add a very important caution: Some of us are privileged to actually see fruit from our labors. We see the growing numbers, bigger budgets, stronger appeal, and the accolades. Others of us, in fact most of us, never see the end result of what God has us doing for Him. So what then? You keep showing up. Keep serving your local church. Keep leading that small group. Remember, God does not measure the success of our ministry by human matrices.

"So how many are you running?" is a common question among senior pastors. Running what? Indeed, God's people are referred to as sheep, but what difference does it really make how many are attending our services? The objective of that question is to measure just how "successful" we are. Here is an inconvenient fact: In God's Kingdom, we do not measure success by numbers, budgets, staff size, or scope of our networks. What we do in the nations as Eagle's Wings International is not better than what a local evangelism ministry in rural Sudan does. We measure ministry success by obedience. The goal is to please Jesus, to please the Master—that's it! We are called to be *pistos*, faithful stewards of the mysteries of Christ.

After we put our heads to the pillow at night, we get to say, "Jesus, thank You that I served You." That's it. I am successful by virtue of my obedience, not my results. It matters not how many people we gather or how big our budget is.

Consider Jesus—three years of ministry; teaching multitudes, feeding thousands, forgiving sins, casting out demons, raising the dead, cleansing lepers, yet how many real followers did He actually have at the end? Here is a hint: *"Then all his disciples deserted him and ran away"* (Mark 14:50 NLT).

How "successful" was Jesus' ministry? Very unsuccessful by human standards.

I enjoy a cherished friendship with a precious couple who are facing a servanthood test right now. God has used them to touch an entire region of the world. They are currently stationed in a country where they are being persecuted by a hostile, racist ministerial establishment. Their reputation has been soiled. Everything inside them is pushing them to strike back, defend, and counterattack. They must die to their reputations. Instead of fighting for their honor, they must accept their estate. They must say, "I am nothing. I am an outlaw, dead to self! I am a *huperetes!*" Failure to do this means disqualification, even if they end up building a big ministry from all of this turmoil.

Gaining Christ often means losing face.

87

Remember Joseph…

God sees this thirteen-year-old kid and thinks, *I want to use him to save My people. He will become the second most important man in all the earth. He will run an empire!* Problem is, Joseph is a bit cocky and lacks discretion. So God sends him to the school of servanthood. First, his brothers sell him into slavery. He joins the lowest of the low. Just as he seems to be thriving in his master's home, Joseph is wrongly convicted of attempted rape, and a second season of suffering ensues. Through adversity, Joseph takes the *Test of Servanthood* to play God's assigned role in the preservation of God's people.

Remember David…

God sends Samuel to anoint a shepherd boy to become the next king of Israel. To equip him for the challenging role, God sends him to the school of servanthood. David served his temperamental mentor, Saul, who turns on him and wants to kill him. While David hides in the caves of Adullum, he must wonder, *Why on earth is this happening, Lord? What happened to Your promises?* David is taking his *Test of Servanthood*.

Let's read again what Paul writes about stewards:

> *Moreover it is required in stewards that one be found faithful* (1 Corinthians 4:2 NKJV).

May God give us ears to hear this and hearts to absorb it. We are low-class, low-life, under-rowers with no entitlements, privileges, prominence, or titles. We are not entitled to anything but a spot in the bottom level of God's galley ship…*huperetes!*

The Test of Reputation

Will you keep rowing even when they throw rocks at you?

Reputation is a summation of how people perceive you. It is a summary of how others see you. The *Test of Reputation* is critical and goes hand in hand with the *Test of Isolation*, Chapter 3. It is almost like the next phase of maturation—now that you don't mind doing ministry alone, can you still do it if you are misjudged or misunderstood?

Friend, if you have never been perceived wrongly, then you have never been seen. In other words, if you have never been wrongly perceived, you have been hiding. As soon as you become visible, you are immediately susceptible to human perception. Unfortunately, people will often misperceive you.

A servant of God must pass this test and must do so conclusively several times over. In other words, this test will come to check your heart throughout the duration of your ministry.

Indeed, the Lord will direct your steps to places of testing and spaces of reputational tension.

A little riddle—what takes you thirty years to build, but can evaporate in thirty minutes? Answer—your reputation. We see this all the time in ministry. Say the wrong words; be at the wrong place; look the wrong way; react improperly, and your life's work can easily blow up in smoke. Critical to our service for the Lord is a sober recognition of this brutal reality.

Authentic servants are content to lay down the right to defend their honor.

PASTOR JAMES

James had faithfully served his community for decades. His neighborhood church was a real beacon of hope to so many. Hundreds had been housed and fed during natural disasters. He had baptized and married all the town's leaders. He volunteered on almost every major initiative and committee. He was a pillar of strength and integrity.

One summer, a reporter claimed to have a bombshell scoop about the now-elderly preacher. A woman had claimed that Pastor James had acted improperly with her decades back. Without corroboration or any fact-checking, the reporter published the salacious article in the Sunday edition of the local newspaper.

The news spread like wildfire. Suddenly it became the biggest scandal the small community had in decades. Within weeks there seemed to be multiple stories of women claiming to have felt uncomfortable with the kind pastor's hugs, warmth, and affections.

James was devastated; his family scandalized. The following month, the board of directors asked him to tender his resignation. Soon after, the town management board, police chaplaincy, and the local Boy Scouts organization did the same thing. His wife had to step down from the women's committee chair and cancel her very popular annual ladies' breakfast. Members started leaving the church. Pastor James was facing a brutal *Test of Reputation.*

Before he does anything else—damage control, press releases, family meetings, etc.—James must first realize that he is a *huperetes*. This reality is vitally important. If he really knows that he is a servant, then he should know that being misunderstood and spoken ill of is part of the proverbial package.

Now I am not suggesting that confronting your accusers and defending yourself is wrong. I am simply challenging the notion that a true servant of the Lord obsesses about how he or she is perceived. Bluntly put, genuine ministers don't care much about what people think about them. When falsely accused, we ought so say, "Ouch that hurts…but hey, I'm an under-rower!"

In some developing countries, it is common to have "house-help," people hired to assist in managing functions such as child rearing, housekeeping, and so on. The house-help are usually comprised of under-privileged gals and guys from upcountry who are normally desperately poor. They are so grateful for the privilege of working for someone who affords them an opportunity to change their circumstances. They will do almost anything so as not to return to their previous environments.

During the course of their employment, it is common, even expected, that house-help will often be misunderstood. Yet you will never hear them say, "What? This is crazy—it's not right. I need to clear my name and defend my reputation!" No, no, no. They are servants; and to the extent they know that, they are content to lay down their right to defend their honor.

VINDICATION

Years ago, someone decided to launch a global campaign to discredit our ministry and destroy my reputation. Much as I tried, the person would not relent. Misinformation was sent around the world, including media outlets and the Internet. It was a dark time for our family and the work of Jesus.

Upon the advisement of well-meaning friends, I fought back, publishing press releases and responding to every inquirer. The more I reacted, the worse it got. I was horrified. "Oh my God… all these people think I am this person! Please help me. Vindicate me and salvage my reputation," I cried.

Friends questioned me. Others believed the reports and broke fellowship with me. Relationships that I had cultivated for years were irreparably broken. I begged for opportunities to present my side of the story. I wanted them to confront me and rebuke me, so I could respond. I hoped that the years of ministry together would somehow tilt the scales in my favor. I was shocked that people who knew me had doubted my character based on an accusation from someone they had never met. I was dumbfounded when they didn't answer my emails or take my calls. I kept thinking, *I can't afford them to see me like this. I have worked too hard to go down like this.*

Suddenly I realized that there was nothing in the world I could do to make the circumstance go away. I was in a place of testing. I was facing a *Test of Reputation*. I began to ponder, *What if they don't believe me? What if they actually walk out of my life completely? What if this relationship is not salvageable?* Then the ultimate question on the test: *What if everyone walks out of my life?* Thankfully I was reminded of Jesus' words:

> *Remember [and continue to remember] that I told you, "A servant is not greater than his master." If they persecuted Me, they will also persecute you. If they kept My word, they will keep yours also* (John 15:20 AMP).

So there is a major terrorist in jail named Barabbas. Seemingly out of the blue, Pilate, the governor of Judea summons him. There are massive crowds all around. Pilate poses a question to the throngs of people, "Do you want me to release Barabbas, or Jesus Christ"? In other words, "Should I let this brutal terrorist back on the streets or this Man who has healed you, raised some of your dead, cleansed lepers, fed thousands of you, and forgiven many of your sins?" And the whole city, the whole community chose Barabbas the terrorist to be freed (Matthew 27:11-26).

Question: If people condemned Jesus, what about me? Basically, if your Lord and Savior was persecuted and spoken ill of, who am I to receive any better treatment? Jesus doesn't say, "Yeah, they might persecute you." Rather He says, *"...they will persecute you"* (John 15:20). It's part of the package. Was Jesus liked by everyone? NO. Was He spoken ill of and maligned? Yes. The *Test of Servanthood* comes to bend your knee; to keep you from forgetting that it is indeed about Jesus—not you. Most importantly, the test's objective is to affirm Christ's lordship over your life.

Anyone who is visible in the ministry
will be attacked.

ECSTATIC

Jesus said:

> *How ecstatic you can be when people insult and persecute you and speak all kinds of cruel lies about you because of your love for me! So leap for joy—since your heavenly reward is great. For you are being rejected the same way the prophets were before you* (Matthew 5:11-12 TPT).

Don't you love this translation of Matthew 5:11-12? Ecstatic? Really, Jesus? Yep…Jesus is advising that when people rise up and attack, discredit, malign, falsely accuse, and lie about us, we are to remain calm. But not only that, to rejoice. In fact, Jesus says, *"leap for joy…."* Why? Because by their attacks, we get to share in the same sufferings of those who have carried the banner of God's Kingdom before us.

Do you know that about 20 percent of people will come against you, regardless of the position you take? In other words, an estimated one in five people will be oppositional to anything new or different. So as ministers, we are called to stand for the cause of Christ in a culture that is demonstrably counter-Christian. No matter if it is Uganda or the Philippines or Russia, the world is trending away from God. If we will stand up and say, "Jesus is Lord, we have to live right," we must expect to be opposed—and if we keep going, expect to be attacked.

Here is what I am really saying: Standing up for Christ triggers opposition. You do not have to be a good person or a gifted person, but simply saying that "Abortion is wrong; lying is wrong; cheating is wrong…and Jesus is Lord, and so expects us to live righteous lives," will stir up opposition and subsequent attacks. They will want to silence you. Bottom line: Standing up for Jesus means standing up to be ridiculed and opposed. That is why Jesus said:

> *So remember what I taught you, that a servant isn't superior to his master. And since they persecuted me, they will also persecute you. And if they obey my teachings, they will also obey yours* (John 15:20 TPT).

There is something called "Christian populism"—the idea that being a Christian is cool. I happen to live in Texas, right in the heartland of the United States "Bible Belt." Here it is common for a radio announcer say, "Make sure you get your tickets to Sunday's game…but remember, y'all gotta go to church!" For Texans, going to church is interwoven into the culture—right up there with owning a handgun.

Jesus said, *"But small is the gate and narrow the road that leads to life, and only a few find it"* (Matthew 7:14 NIV). It seems to me that some of us are trying to make the gateway to the narrow road glittery and glamorous with sparkling lights. We want to make Jesus attractive and cool. We want "seekers" to think, *Oh, Christianity is easy. I like going to church. It inspires me to become a better person.* All seems well until they begin to really walk the narrow road to serve Jesus. They realize just how thorny and rugged the narrow road really is—that Jesus is not so cool after all, and that authentic ministry causes social ostracism and persecution is part of the package. Then they feel duped and lied to because they were promised a cool Jesus.

"My boss is really persecuting me," pleaded one brother.

"Oh, really?! Is it because you read the Bible or because you are preaching too much at work?"

"No!" he gasped. "He knows I'm a Christian, but he seems to be discriminating against me because he won't promote me!"

"Sorry, brother," I said. "Your boss is picking on you because he does not like your work ethic or personality type, but I would not call that persecution!"

Persecution is not when someone doesn't like you. Persecution is when you are attacked because of your love for Jesus. It is when your family attacks you because you enrolled into ministry training school instead of going to law school. It is when your father disowns you for becoming a pastor and shaming the family (see Matthew 5:11).

As a *huperetes*, you and I get to *"Rejoice and be glad, because great is your reward in heaven..."* (Matthew 5:12 NIV).

The Message Bible says the same verse this way, *"You can be glad when that happens—give a cheer, even!—for though they don't like it, I do! And all heaven applauds."*

And why should we rejoice? Because we *"know that you are in good company. My prophets and witnesses have always gotten into this kind of trouble"* (Matthew 5:12 MSG).

If nobody has ever attacked you for your passion for Christ, then you've probably never been visible. Love Jesus hard enough, and someday somebody will attack you for it. Expressed convictions trigger attacks. This is the *Test of Reputation*, and it must be passed.

Real ministers acquire a taste for the cup of persecution.

ENEMIES

Thou preparest a table before me in the presence of mine enemies... (Psalm 23:5).

Now we like that promise, but hardly take time to think about its full meaning.

Before we dine, there are enemies. Who is an enemy? Someone committed to your humiliation or destruction. Sometimes an enemy will benefit you way more than even a friend. Dennis, how can you say that? In my winding forty-year journey with the Lord, God has used my enemies to transition me. I see them at every turn of my ministry.

A few examples...

God used an enemy to move me from my birth home of Uganda to London, England, in 1989. Years later, He would use another enemy to transition me from a recording artist into a music missionary. In 2004, the Lord would use an enemy to push me into Christian education and ministry training. He used another enemy to evict me from a comfortable position in a megachurch into pastoral ministry in Chicago. Three years later, an enemy was sent to launch me into global apostolic ministry.

Now, did I ask for these toxic people to be sent into my life to inflict such unspeakable pain? Of course not. They lied about me, attacked my character, and maligned my reputation. They relentlessly persecuted me. I hurt. I wept. I pleaded and begged that God would vindicate me. He didn't. Instead, He prepared a banquet table and invited me to dine, right in front of them. Even more importantly, along with an eviction notice from that season, each of them carried an exam for the *Test of Reputation*. I had to firmly answer this question: Will you keep going, keep rowing, even when they throw rocks at you?

Consider Joseph again…

He is a beloved last born of his powerful dad, Jacob. God begins to show Joseph that there was more inside of him than just being a daddy's boy. His jealous brothers become enemies, determined to kill him. God uses them to evict him from a comfortable homelife into slavery. Favor comes upon him and the next thing he knows, he is prosperous and living in a wealthy Egyptian's home. Suddenly an enemy is born in Potiphar's wife. She is used to thrust Joseph into an Egyptian prison. If He had spoken to his no-doubt confused servant, God would have said something like, "Joseph, hold steady. I am evicting you to promote you." But He didn't. So there is Joseph in jail, feeling forgotten, until one day when he goes from prisoner to running the most powerful kingdom in the world.

Consider David again…

Look at David, a lowly shepherd boy. God used a giant enemy bent on killing him to elevate him from the back hills to the king's courts. Then the man he loves, Saul, turns on him and becomes his vicious enemy. Next, he is hiding in the caves. Unknowingly, it is Saul's enmity that ultimately catapults David to the throne.

Where is your enemy? Don't be too quick to curse or pray them way. Embrace the attacks. Don't fight back. Stay dead to yourself and alive in Jesus. Jesus said:

...Except a corn of wheat fall into the ground and die, it abideth alone: but if it die, it bringeth forth much fruit (John 12:24).

How do you know you are dead? By what you do when you are attacked, lied about, defamed, insulted, discredited, persecuted. How you respond is a measure of how dead you are. Take your emotional temperature when you get slandered or misunderstood. How do you sleep at night knowing that your church or Christian friends are thinking a certain wrong way about you? How do you respond to a rumor you cannot quench?

> *The way you react to attacks is a measure of how dead you are.*

Whether it's an attack from your small group or a slanderous article in a local newspaper, this test will challenge us all the same. Let me leave you with this amazing report from Dr. Luke concerning the early believers:

The apostles left the high council rejoicing that God had counted them worthy to suffer disgrace for the name of Jesus (Acts 5:41 NLT).

This is not a feel-good test. It does not feel good when you suffer disgrace, but it is an honor. In fact, I would challenge every believer to desire this blessing. Can you imagine standing in line and saying, "Me Lord, send me some of that disgrace!" Crazy, right?

"But Dennis, God wants to bless us," someone might say. Indeed, He does. God wants to bless you, but can you take the whole package? Peace, favor, joy, health, promotions...and persecution? Many of us think blessing means having more, better, bigger. This is a distortion injected into our theology by the enemy. It is a fact that we can be blessed and still be in want of health and earthly resources. In other words, you can be blessed and still not have enough.

Blessed are those who are persecuted... (Matthew 5:10).

When attacked, those who have embraced this blessing will say, "Hallelujah, I rejoice in You, Lord. They just talked about me really badly...people I love are spreading ugly lies about me; but even still, I am blessed."

Does it hurt? Yes. Do you cry? Sometimes. Do you wish to go out and set the record straight? Do you want to draft a memo, text, or email to really explain your heart and clear you name? Absolutely. But you don't always have to, or get to. Instead, you let them think and say what they will about you. You chose to lay it all down and die. You take the blessing. You pass the test because you are a *huperetes!*

Are you facing the dreadful *Test of Reputation* today? Pray this with me:

Father, my flesh screams at the notion of being misunderstood, discredited, or talked about in a way that is not right or fair. And oh the urge to set the record straight, to enlighten my attackers, and explain my innocence to any listening ear. God, will You please grant me the grace to shut up, and then the grace to endure? But all the more, Lord, grant me the grace to rejoice, knowing that blessings shall be unleashed upon me. In Jesus' matchless name. Amen.

CHAPTER 6

The Test of Time

Will you keep rowing after the sun sets?

First, let's unpack the concept of time, which I call God's unmerited gift.

Time is one thing that you didn't ask for but cannot lose or give away. Whereas you might lose your health, all your money, family, or marriage, the one resource that cannot be lost is time. We all have twenty-four hours from one sunset to another, period! You are not going to wake up tomorrow and hear God say, "Okay My child, because you have been less than obedient, today I will give you only twenty hours." Never!

Time is also irreplaceable. The proverbial clock does not turn back for anyone, regardless of your status or net worth. When time rolls forward, it is gone, forever. There will never be another January 22, 2020.

And here is another fascinating truth. Although you can recover your health, dig yourself out of debt, make new friends, jumpstart a dead career, remarry and start a new family, time, once it passes, is either spent wisely or it is wasted, squandered, and cannot be redeemed. It is infinitely more valuable than all other earthly possessions.

Time is life's most perishable commodity.

I was born in a small Ugandan village called Mukono. At the time, Uganda was the poorest country in that region, thirteenth from the bottom in fact. I remember thinking, *Man, I wish I was born in London.* I also remember the simple, yet profound thought, *Well, I can't help that I was born here. But just like the Europeans have twenty-four hours to live, so have I.* I had unwittingly stumbled upon this timeless truth—as far as time is concerned, we are all born equal. I began to see time as a great leveler. What I did with it would determine my destiny.

A TOOL

In my book *You Have a Dream*, I write:

God Himself uses time to equip men and women for the future that He has prepared for them. It's His investment tool! For example, He invested eighty years of training in Moses before he became the mighty leader we know. Our Lord Jesus invested thirty years to prepare for a three-and-a-half-year ministry. God used the past four decades in Uganda, England, and the USA to prepare me for the global ministry I have today. I often draw from the wisdom that I have gleaned during the seasons of dryness, plowing, and plenty that I have endured and enjoyed throughout the years. God used time to make me the man I am today.

It was not until he turned forty years old that Moses realized his destiny. He hastily tried to execute it by killing an Egyptian. Clearly, he wasn't ready. He was much too impulsive and emotional. I can almost hear the Lord say, "Okay, son...I know you get it now, but we need to work on you some more. I am going to put you in this vast desert place called Sinai. You will stay here as long as you need to develop the temperament of a servant-leader." Moses would spend forty years in obscurity. I bet you that ten years in, at age 50, he probably felt ready. But he wasn't. God needed another thirty years to skill His servant.

Back to Joseph again. Joseph is a teenager, Daddy's boy, and a dreamer. Trouble is, he has no discretion. He humiliates everybody with his dreams, causing dissent among his brothers, and really needs conditioning for the vital assignment ahead. So God takes the tool of time, thirteen years, to fashion an impulsive young man into a statesman and prime minister in the most powerful kingdom on the earth.

After being anointed the next king of Israel by Samuel, young David is no doubt feeling pretty good until Dad says, "Well, that was a surprise. Time to get back to the sheep, son." David was not the favorite. He had an unfortunate history, so he was an unlikely candidate for this divine appointment to be the king.

After Samuel leaves, God needs to employ His instrument of time to prepare the young apprentice for the historic role ahead. Indeed He does, and He takes fourteen years to do it. From Saul's palace to the caves of Adullam, the young, immature shepherd boy named David is transformed into Israel's greatest king!

Think about the thirty years of molding God used to mature John the Baptist for his six-month ministry. Concerning him, Jesus said:

> *I tell you the truth, of all who have ever lived, none is greater than John the Baptist...* (Matthew 11:11 NLT).

What about our Lord Jesus Christ? The Bible says:

> *But even though he was a wonderful Son, he learned to listen and obey through all his sufferings* (Hebrews 5:8 TPT).

To do this, God took time—three decades—to equip Jesus for the greatest mission in all of history.

And after Paul had his Damascus Road experience in Acts chapter 9, it took fourteen years of transformation before the Holy Spirit separated him for ministry as written about in Acts chapter 13.

I have mentored many a young man who have said, "Sir, I'm ready. I want to go into full-time ministry right now. I am ready to serve God wherever He leads me." And I am thinking, *Umm... not so fast. You don't know how to follow yet. Plus, you keep thinking everything is about you.* Time must work on the young lad.

Becoming has a price tag—time.

Paul encourages the Galatian believers:

> *And let us not grow weary while doing good, for in **due season** we shall reap if we do not lose heart* (Galatians 6:9 NKJV).

The Message Bible translation puts it this way:

*So let's not allow ourselves to get fatigued doing good. At the right **time** we will harvest a good crop if we don't give up or quit.*

Friend, your present life station is a direct result of time investments into your journey. If you want to grow, make new friends, get healthy, and mature in the Lord, it will cost you the currency of time.

THE OVEN

Can you withstand this sometimes-brutal instrument of time long enough for God to incubate the gift that He has placed inside of you? And just so you know, it will almost always take longer than you expected. Humans always feel like God is late. Every man or woman of God who has ever been used by God had the feeling that God was delayed, that He takes too long.

The *Test of Time* poses this key question: Will you allow God to form in you the person He has in His mind, or are you going to panic and launch prematurely?

When God spoke to me at age thirteen that He would use me in the nations, I had absolutely no idea what it meant. My family was impoverished, and the nation was mired by political violence. The loftiest I could dream was a trip to neighboring Kenya. He did not tell me it would take three years before I landed an invitation to travel on a fourteen-hour bus drive to Nairobi, Kenya, for a conference. It would take six years before we were invited to visit a church group in London, England, where this ministry to the nations was launched.

Paul is incarcerated in a Roman jail. His ministry has already impacted the spread of Christianity. I am sure he has a long list of invitations from young churches across Asia minor and Europe. Instead, he is stuck in a jail cell writing letters. Paul was eventually martyred, but wow has God used those letters to touch people's lives for centuries! They have been read by billions around the world, thus fulfilling his destiny to take the Gospel to the Gentiles. Paul writes:

I am a special messenger from Christ Jesus to you Gentiles. I bring you the Good News so that I might present you as an acceptable offering to God, made holy by the Holy Spirit. So I have reason to be enthusiastic about all Christ Jesus has done through me in my service to God. Yet I dare not boast about anything except what Christ has done through me, bringing the Gentiles to God by my message and by the way I worked among them (Romans 15:16-18 NLT).

Yes…that was the plan; it was why Paul was born. But the path led through incarceration, jail, prison, and an ultimately death. And all of that took time.

Paul advised the Galatians:

So let's not allow ourselves to get fatigued doing good. At the right time we will harvest a good crop if we don't give up, or quit (Galatians 6:9 MSG).

For the more than twelve years that I served as a full-time missionary evangelist and international recording artist, my job often involved many hours on airplanes flying across continents. I experienced very long layovers and entire days in hotel rooms away from my family. On several occasions I flew more than 10,000 miles to sing a couple of songs in an evangelistic crusade or music festival.

One day I decided that instead of reading entertainment magazines and Christian novels, playing video games, or renting DVDs to help me pass the idle time on the road, I would read growth literature and listen to motivational materials. I used all those hundreds of hours to earn an education. God used this time to equip me for the mandate He had given me.

I often tell proteges, "If your aim is to grow a weed, you only need twenty-four hours. If you wish to grow a squash, you need three months; a pineapple, one year; an oak tree, seven long years." Friend, if God intends to do something big inside of you, He will use the wonderful instrument of time.

Yet you, Lord, are our Father. We are the clay, you are the potter; we are all the work of your hand (Isaiah 64:8 NIV).

Imagine you are in an oven, God's oven. Every so often, He smilingly looks at you through the oven door to check if it's time to get you out.

"Can I get out now? Surely I'm ready," you lament.

"Umm," He gently ponders, "Nah...I need you to be browner. You are not yet done, My child." And He painfully pulls away.

You do not see yourself because you are not in the mind of the Potter. Only He knows how long to leave you there. Only He knows what He is making. Now here is the problem: there is always a disparity between your time and your neighbor's time in the kiln. Because God doesn't make replicas, the temperatures and durations differ from vessel to vessel. A decorative pot doesn't require the same amount of heat as a water pot. The latter needs to be much stronger as it is destined to endure more usage.

Similarly, God will, without explanation, often remove your neighbor from the kiln ahead of you. So you think, *Hey, what about me, Lord? I should get out now too, right?* Not necessarily. Your job as a Kingdom leader is to conform to the infinitely intelligent design of the omniscient Potter.

Your job as a vessel is to conform to the pattern that is in the mind of the Potter.

James writes:

> *Consider it a sheer gift, friends, when tests and challenges come at you from all sides. You know that under pressure, your faith-life is forced into the open and shows its true colors. So don't try to get out of anything prematurely. Let it do its work so you become mature and well-developed, not deficient in any way* (James 1:4 MSG).

Let me tell you about a really interesting plant called the Chinese bamboo tree. For five years, the tree shows no signs of growth. Zero. Can you imagine that? Farmers literally work on bamboo tree plantations for five years with no visible growth. Then suddenly, the bamboo tree begins to grow. Wait…that's not all. It grows a shocking 90 feet tall in a period of six weeks.

Question: Do you think that the bamboo plant is stagnated and dormant for five years? Not at all. While we don't see any progress above ground, the Chinese bamboo plant is growing an extensive root system without which it cannot support the gargantuan height, as you can appreciate.

Are you feeling suspended, stagnated on one of life's deserted stations? Does it seem like God is passing you by, promoting others around you? Does it look like everyone else is growing except you? Don't despair. Consider that you are growing roots for the windy days ahead. When people pull on you, use you, move on, leave your church, and your kindness is rewarded with betrayal and abandonment, you'll be glad you waited your five years to grow roots.

And don't allow yourselves to be weary or disheartened in planting good seeds, for the season of reaping the wonderful harvest you've planted is coming! (Galatians 6:9 TPT)

Paul advises the Galatians not to despair from the often longer-than-anticipated wait that accompanies ministerial sowing. We give; we travail for peoples' breakthroughs, expecting some kind of tangible reward. We want everyone to be free, delivered, and prosperous. Instead, the opposite is often true. They fall away. Some betray and even attack us, leaving us confused, discouraged, and despondent, asking, "Lord, what happened?"

In my book *You have a Dream*, I write:

Says M. Scott Peck, "Until you value yourself, you won't value your time. Until you value your time, you will not do anything with it." Once you grasp this concept, you will be able to manage your time effectively, and thus also your life. You will be able to wisely invest this highly perishable and priceless resource of time to accelerate your walk toward your God-given dream. The Bible says: *"Hard work means prosperity; **only a fool idles away his time**"* (Proverbs 12:11 TLB). In other words, whereas wise people spend or exchange their time for prosperity and increase, foolish people waste it, squander it, and misspend it. Observes Charles Spezzano, "You don't really pay for things with money. You pay for them with time. 'In five years, I'll have put enough money away to buy a vacation house we want. Then I will slow down.' That means the house will cost you five years—one-twelfth of your adult life. Translate the dollar value of the house, car, or anything else into time, and then see if it's still worth it. The phrase 'spending your time' is not a metaphor. It's how life works."

May this be our prayer today: Lord…

Teach us to realize the brevity of life [to make the most of our time], *so that we may grow in wisdom* (Psalm 90:12 NLT).

Our days and nights are made up of time. The prayer could be stated this way, "Lord, teach us to manage our time, that we may apply our hearts to Your wisdom."

I am writing this chapter as I watch my son, Judah, spin around in a gymnasium on a chilly Texas night. These thoughts constantly run through my mind: Is this what I am supposed to be doing right now? Ingrid could come watch him while I run some errands. I could just leave him here and go catch up on the latest political news. I could go home and pack for our upcoming Africa trip, or make a counseling call.

Then I calm my soul and whisper that prayer: "Lord, teach me to number my days. Teach me to manage my time." See, this day will never come back. These hours will not be given back to me. Woe is me if I squander them.

Notice that it says, *"our time."* That's right…not theirs, but our time! It is the unmerited, undeserved 168 hours each week for which we must ultimately give an account. How others spend their time is really not our business. We steward our time because that is what has been gifted to us.

God has given you a voice that no one else has. That is why it is a tragedy when we spend our lives echoing others. Because there can only be one voice. Think about the late Reverend Billy Graham, for example. Fortunately his son, Franklin, realized years ago that he could not be his dad. Subsequently, there is only one Franklin Graham. How tragic would it be if Franklin Graham spent decades of his life trying to be his dad.

I do not want any of my children to become clones of me. The same applies to everyone I am honored to mentor or pastor. Flattering as it is to hear, "Wow, Dr. Dennis, I want to be just like you," it's also deeply troubling to me. I honestly feel like if I succeeded in making them like me, the world would miss being blessed with what God has placed inside them.

Whereas Paul invites the Corinthians to imitate him as he imitated Christ, we know that ultimately his journey was different from theirs. All my heroes have told me about the imitation stages of their journey where they emulated or even mimicked ministers they admired. But sooner or later, they had to find their own voices.

The echoes must find their voices.

So I pose this question in conclusion: *Huperetes*…will you sit contently with yourself until God is done with you? Will you endure the sometimes-boring, sometimes-mundane, sometimes-monotonous, sometimes-draining process of the making of a pleasing vessel? Will you pass the *Test of Time?*

CHAPTER 7

The Test of Success

Will you keep rowing even after you reach the summit of your mountain?

Here is a disruptive thought: a pastor or ministry leader is not called to be successful in the common sense of the word. Here is why…success is a secular idea because it is based on some human matrix like net worth or notoriety. In other words, people are considered successful when they attain a certain level of measurable achievement.

For example, a church is considered successful when it reaches a certain number of members or patrons, or when it reaches financial viability. Megachurches are considered successful because they can attract or serve thousands of people. Indeed, many have attained financial success and produced some of the most famous speakers and authors, but a good number of them are crippled with compromise, abuse, and toxic theology. Is that success?

I am certainly not suggesting that all megachurches are bad. I am only using them as a clear example of visible success.

But this question bears asking: Is a small neighborhood church with a dual-income senior pastor and no paid stuff less successful?

"Pray for us, Dr. Dennis," begged a young leader at the end of a church growth workshop where I had spoken. "We are stuck at two hundred members," he lamented. "When I look at big churches like this one, I feel like a loser. We really need a breakthrough." For four days, this young minister had heard stories of massive feeding programs, million-dollar media campaigns, and mind-blowing illustrated messaging from some of America's megachurch pastors. Compared to his small-town church congregation of farmers, he was an abject failure.

"How big is your town?" I quizzed.

"Around four thousand."

"Well, my brother, unless the Lord moves you to a much larger town or gives you another pastorate in another state altogether, it is unlikely that you will ever pastor a conventional megachurch, which has to have at least 2,500 members."

He looked dumbfounded. "But why? I really want to do more for our community. I want to build a magnificent structure like this one and serve our town."

I looked him squarely in the eye and said, "Pastor, you are standing in a multimillion-dollar structure in a city of nine million people. Comparing apples to apples, your 200-member church in a city of 4,000 is statistically larger than this church. Five percent of your community comes to your church. That is huge! If these guys had those numbers here in Chicago, this church would have 450,000 members, 5 percent of the total population. Or to put it in another way, if this church was in your town, it would have eight members." His face lit up!

That pastor felt discouraged because he was using a flawed human matrix to measure ministerial success. Realistically speaking, he will probably always be bi-vocational and will never run a multimillion-dollar ministry complex with state-of-the-art, high-definition television cameras and sports courts for his community.

We are called to obedience, not success.

Consider our predecessors Peter, James, John, Simon, Bartholomew, even Paul. Do you think these guys would be considered successful through the lens of today's prism for ministerial success? At the height of their ministries, they were disgraced and mocked; a band of misfits who were murdered mercilessly. And we have the audacity to use their writings to teach that ministry is synonymous with glamour.

When you say, "Jesus, use me!" you are enlisting into a life of toil, a life of sweat, displeasure, betrayals, no pillow at night—yet somehow through the tears you smile. Because you know this is it! This is what you have chosen to do. And if given the opportunity you would choose it again.

STEWARDS

Paul writes:

Let a man so account of us, as of the ministers of Christ, and stewards of the mysteries God (1 Corinthians 4:1).

The Greek word for "steward" is *oikonomos*, which means a household manager or caretaker. You and I are caretakers of the mysteries of God. What does that really mean? Plainly put, that church or ministry is not yours. Your gifts, talents, wisdom, and abilities to serve Jesus do not belong to you. The supernatural wisdom to solve problems, to point direction, to provide critical guidance or give prophetic insight…all of that is not ours. It is His. We only get to manage it. We are each an *oikonomos*.

Quite often I bump into ministers who seem to think that because God is using them, they must be something super-special. I hear statements such as:

"I am a gift to the Body of Christ."

"My ministry is needed here."

"You all need to be under my covering."

Deception…

Every other week, someone will say, "Wow, Dr. Dennis you've changed my life." Or, "Our marriage would have collapsed had you not come into our lives." Or, "God used you to restore my family." Or, "I am alive because of you!" Sincere hearts touched by the Lord, but certainly not me. For a fact, I cannot change a life, heal a marriage, break an addiction, or destroy a single cancer cell. Granted they came to one of our events where I was used as a conduit by the Holy Spirit to deliver or heal or speak into their lives, but I cannot lose sight of the fact that He did it! Not me alone. Paul writes:

> *For to one is given the word of wisdom through the Spirit, to another the word of knowledge by the same Spirit, to another faith by the same Spirit, to another the gifts of healings*

by the same Spirit, to another the working of miracles, to another prophecy, to another discerning of spirits, to another different kinds of tongues, to another the interpretation of tongues (1 Corinthians 12:8-10 NKJV).

I have been blessed to walk in all these gifts in various seasons of my winding ministry journey. They are gifts. I didn't do anything special to get them. I did not have to be more spiritual than my peers to be given these gifts. Paul adds:

It is the one and only Spirit who distributes all these gifts. He alone decides which gift each person should have (1 Corinthians 12:11 NLT).

The Holy Spirit decided to gift them to me of His own volition for service in the execution of the Great Commission. Again, they are not for me to use to manipulate or for any self-gain. I don't even know how they work. Honestly speaking, even though I have been chosen to use these gifts for four decades, I do not, for example, fully understand how I can share certain words and sinners begin to weep as they give their hearts to Jesus.

I just don't have that kind of power. How can I possibly know that a particular injury someone experienced at five years old is responsible for their current trauma, or that someone was raped last year but had told no one. I couldn't possibly know how to lead a grown man back to the place of childhood trauma, get him free from that emotional imprint, and lead him to complete freedom in Christ. How does that work? I don't know, but it's really none of my business. As a *huperetes*, I am merely a steward, a caretaker of the mysteries of God.

Friend, the workings of God are mysterious, and mysterious they must remain; wonderful and so must they remain; marvelous and so must they remain; glorious and so must they remain, and awesome and so must they remain…or we become too familiar with them. Here is now I like to put it—if we attempt to make them understandable, sensible, or reasonable, then this becomes just another philosophy, another religion.

Demystify the mysteries of Christ, and you create an impotent faith.

ZOOM OUT

As a ministry, we do not just visit places for preaching opportunities. We don't book engagements to simply populate our calendar. Today I never look at ministry in the short-term. I am zoomed out, all the time looking at the wider long-term perspective. This is something I had to learn.

I remember when my friends and I first met my late spiritual dad, Dr. Myles Munroe, in Accra, Ghana. As soon as we were done with the pleasantries, Dr. Munroe asked, "So guys, exactly where do you see your ministry in ten years?"

Ten years? What on earth is he talking about? Who plans that far ahead? I thought. We were perplexed. *Maybe he needs to see our biography,* I thought. He needs to know what Limit X has accomplished. He needs to know how busy we are. He needs to see our itinerary.

I fumbled to answer his question, but clearly had no clue. As we parted, he hugged us and said, "Sons, think and plan ahead. Your very future depends on it."

For the next few days I thought long and hard. What Papa Munroe wanted to know was if we had taken the time to zoom out. He would later say to me, "Son, if you cannot see the ultimate, you become enslaved to the immediate."

The concept was not entirely new to us. Soon after our music group, Limit X, went into full-time ministry in the early 1990s, we began having what we liked to call dream sessions. We talked about a soon-coming day when we would be booked all around the world. We saw our music selling globally and imagined sharing stages with some of the people we admired. We saw a global ministry, even before we had a single booking. We zoomed out.

As a result, whenever an opportunity or door opened before us, we asked ourselves if pursuing it would bring us closer to our vision or push us further away. Looking back at those early years, this one factor helped us succeed against seemingly insurmountable odds.

When God transitioned me into itinerant ministry in 2007, I was determined to never lose sight of the mission at hand. I wrote strict codes of ethics to help guide me through the dangerous terrain of global ministry. I looked over the fence and decided I would not be for sale. I was not going to issue contracts or charge speaking fees to my hosts. I was going to obey God and go where He sent me without any requirements or preconditions. Eagle's Wings International was going to be funded without manipulation or gimmicks.

If God really called me, He would finance His work. I also refused to build a ministry based on charisma, personality, or giftings. I decided never to exaggerate numbers or inflate the impact of our work. I knew that choosing this route would mean that I would never be as popular or "big" as some of my peers, but we would do God's work with integrity and honor. I was determined to be driven by my purpose. And God has honored this commitment.

The Bible says:

Where there is no vision, the people perish… (Proverbs 29:18).

In place of the word "perish," the New Living Translation uses the phrase *"they run wild."*

If you don't zoom out, you become consumed with immediate gratification.

The New International Version of the same Scripture says:

Where there is no revelation, the people cast off restraint.…

The pastor who manipulates the congregation loses sight of the call of God on his life and casts off all restraint—enslaved by the temporary pleasure of the moment.

In Genesis 25:29-34 (AMP) we read:

Jacob had cooked [reddish-brown lentil] stew [one day], when Esau came from the field and was famished; and Esau said to Jacob, "Please, let me have a quick swallow of that red stuff there, because I am exhausted and famished." For that reason Esau was [also] called Edom (Red). Jacob answered, "First sell me your birthright (the rights of a first-born)." Esau said, "Look, I am about to die [if I do not eat soon]; so of what use is this birthright to me?" Jacob said, "Swear [an oath] to me today [that you are selling it to me for this food]"; so he swore [an oath] to him, and sold him his birthright. Then Jacob gave Esau bread and lentil stew;

and he ate and drank, and got up and went on his way. In this way Esau scorned his birthright.

What a tragic story! Esau sold his birthright for a temporary need, a hearty meal, trading his future for momentary pleasure. He literally exchanged his destiny for a bowl of red lentil stew. Clearly, he was a man who had cast off restraint and not zoomed out! The blind author and entrepreneur Helen Keller said, "What's worse than being blind is having sight without vision." How powerful!

When I speak along these lines, some of my fellow ministers say, "Dennis, I don't want to figure God out. He will do what He wants done." Sadly, I have seen countless ministries destroyed by this misguided attitude. Many a believer has quit a job prematurely thinking that God was calling him or her to immediate full-time ministry. Many a pastor has ruined a church because a major building project or TV ministry was launched before the pastor was ready.

At the beginning of every year, my wife and I sit down and ask, "What do we want to accomplish as a family this year?" We carefully define our spiritual, social, financial, family, and personal targets and goals for the year. We zoom out. Then, for the next twelve months, we enjoy the adventure.

The Bible tells us:

The prudent understand where they are going, but fools deceive themselves (Proverbs 14:8 NLT).

A *huperetes* could not afford to focus on the temporary if he was going to survive down in the ugly bottom gully of the ship. He had to zoom out.

Many times I have looked back on a twelve-day tour in a country, only to realize that the highlights were not the public events, but the drive with a hungry young leader, or the young woman who laments, "Dr. Dennis, I feel called to the ministry but need to decide whether to wait to get married first or just pack my bags and go!" In fact, oftentimes, my greatest meetings are the smallest ones.

PISTOS

Moreover it is required in stewards that one be found faithful (1 Corinthians 4:2 NKJV).

The Greek word for "faithful" in this verse is *pistos*, which means trustworthy.

A few years back, I had the honor of taking Dr. Mary Alice and Dr. Kurt Schroeder on a European mission trip with me. I affectionately call them Papa and Mama Kurt. Although we ministered in numerous public events in Sweden and Switzerland, it was the long breakfast meetings, the long car rides, and the late-night, fast-food stops at deserted gas stations that I cherished the most.

I saw what a godly marriage looks like after fifty-five years together. I saw an accomplished man of valor. I sat with a father to so many apprentices and spiritual sons and daughters as we talked about his conquests and triumphs. We discussed his health challenges, disillusionments with some churches and the Body of Christ in general, mistakes, missteps, and regrets.

Is Papa Kurt successful? Consider this: Papa walks with a limp from a bout with childhood polio. Over the years, hundreds of some of the most powerful healing gifts in the Body of Christ including Kathryn Kuhlman, the Hunters, and others have prayed for his leg to be healed. His church, Goodnews Center, has hosted renowned healing revivalists from Bethel and all the seven major revival movements dating as far back to the Jesus Movement. By now, he should be cynical and maybe faithless concerning God ever healing him. But guess what…he isn't.

One evening on our trip, God's power started healing people. "Sir, may I pray for you?" asked one of the young people. "Yes," replied Papa Kurt gleefully. "Come on, let's go!" "I believe you will be healed today," announced the young apprentice. Other kids joined in, loudly praying in tongues.

"Is it healed?" they quizzed.

"No, it is not," he responded.

About an hour later, we could see discouragement on their faces. Finally, the group leader resigns, "Man…it didn't work."

"That's ok. I needed that!" Papa Kurt graciously responded.

As we drove home that evening, I asked what he thought about the young kids praying for his leg. "Hey, you never know if today is that day, Dennis! Maybe God uses that kid and not those great healing evangelists. I keep thinking, maybe next time!" That is what I call true success. Papa Kurt has this uncanny ability to keep his heart pure through his brutal journey of faith and ministry.

Then there is Mama Mary Alice, his wife, a prophetess indeed. "I made a pledge to the Lord," Mama said. "The man who first kisses me is the one I will marry." So there is young Kurt and Mary Alice gathered to pray for their city back in the day. Naughty Kurt has a thought, *I want to kiss her lips.* So with her eyes closed in prayer, he reaches in and kisses her. She is shocked and outraged because all feelings aside, she made a pledge. Now she has to marry him. And she did, suspending her dreams of being a missionary to the nations until she joined our ministry forty years later. She is one of the most love-filled women I have ever met. With all the vast experiences they have had serving with historic generals in God's Kingdom, you'd think they have "seen it all." On the contrary, they are incredible students of life and ministry. They have passed the *Test of Success!*

What is success? It does not have to be more or bigger. It does not have to be lateral or movement upward. Success sometimes looks like a demotion.

God measures success by faithfulness.

Consider Joseph again. One day he is a respected steward in Potiphar's home—the next day, he is in jail. Unbeknown to him, he is closer to his ultimate assignment, but it absolutely doesn't feel like it.

For example, say you need to travel to the next mountain up yonder but between you and the mountain is a deep valley. When you get to the valley, you are actually closer to your destination, although you are not as high as you were previously.

This test is about this question: Can you keep a gentle soul even after you climb the mountain? Keep this in mind: God does not measure success by numbers, clout, networks, popularity, likes, clicks, or hits.

PAPA ABRAHAM

Abraham is seventy-five years old when he receives God's first promise:

Now the Lord had said to Abram: "Get out of your country, from your family, and from your father's house, to a land that I will show you" (Genesis 12:1 NKJV).

Basically, leave your country and your family and move to a place I will show you. And then the second part of the promise from God is in the following verse:

I will make you a great nation; I will bless you and make your name great; and you shall be a blessing (Genesis 12:2 NKJV).

That was promise number one.

Five years later after Abram has almost dropped the ball by not obeying God's instruction to leave everyone behind because he took his cousin Lot with him, we read:

Then the Lord appeared to Abram and said, "I will give this land to your descendants…" (Genesis 12:7 NLT).

That was the second promise to Abram from God.

So everything is good until Abram faces the *Test of Conviction* when a great famine hits the land. He goes off to Egypt, trades his gorgeous sixty-five-year-old wife to the mighty Pharaoh in exchange for freedom, sheep, goats, cattle, donkeys, servants, and camels. The Bible says that *"Abram was very rich in cattle, in silver and gold"* (Genesis 13.2 NLT).

After a bitter feud with his cousin, the Lord says:

And I will give you so many descendants that, like the dust of the earth, they cannot be counted! Go and walk through the land in every direction, for I am giving it to you (Genesis 13:16-17 NLT).

That was promise number three.

Shortly thereafter, the Lord says:

> *Do not be afraid, Abram, for I will protect you, and your reward will be great* (Genesis 15:1 NLT).

That was promise number four.

As the years roll on, Abram is antsy. He is blessed, but afraid that maybe God is somehow mistaken about the sequence of the promise. Will he be alive long enough to produce an heir? Perhaps his male servant Eliezer will inherit his wealth.

> *Then the Lord said to him, "No, your servant will not be your heir, for you will have a son of your own who will be your heir." Then the Lord took Abram outside and said to him, "Look up into the sky and count the stars if you can. That's how many descendants you will have!"* (Genesis 15:4-5 NLT)

That was promise number five.

So God cuts a covenant with Abram; He prophesies four hundred years of captivity right there in Egypt and the eventual deliverance of His people.

Meanwhile, Sarai, his wife, is watching. She is unsure about her ability to have babies. So she suggests Abram should take a shortcut. Rather than leave his wealth to Eliezer, Abram darling should take one of her fine girl servants, Hagar.

When Abram agrees, right then he fails the *Test of Time*. He capitulates and bears a son with Hagar, who mistreats Sarai, who turns around and blames Abram for the whole fiasco. Abram's response: *"Look, she is your servant, so deal with her as you see fit"*

(Genesis 16:6 NLT). Abram basically doesn't want to deal with it. Maybe it's his ripe age of eighty-six that prompts this resigned response. To paraphrase, he says, "You know what? She's your servant. Throw her out, cast her away, whatever you want to do… she's yours."

After Hagar's son, Ishmael, is born, God goes quiet for the next thirteen years.

> *When Abram was ninety-nine years old, the Lord appeared to him and said, "I am El-Shaddai—'God Almighty.' Serve me faithfully and live a blameless life. I will make a covenant with you, by which I will guarantee to give you countless descendants." At this, Abram fell face down on the ground. Then God said to him, "This is my covenant with you: I will make you the father of a multitude of nations! What's more, I am changing your name. It will no longer be Abram. Instead, you will be called Abraham, for you will be the father of many nations"* (Genesis 17:1-5 NLT).

That was promise number six.

Next, God speaks a covenant of circumcision.

> *Then God said to Abraham, "Regarding Sarai, your wife— her name will no longer be Sarai. From now on her name will be Sarah. And I will bless her and give you a son from her! Yes, I will bless her richly, and she will become the mother of many nations. Kings of nations will be among her descendants." Then Abraham bowed down to the ground, but he laughed to himself in disbelief. "How could I become a father at the age of 100?" he thought. "And how can Sarah have a baby when she is ninety years old?" So Abraham said to God, "May Ishmael live under your special blessing!"*

But God replied, "No—Sarah, your wife, will give birth to a son for you. You will name him Isaac, and I will confirm my covenant with him and his descendants as an everlasting covenant. As for Ishmael, I will bless him also, just as you have asked. I will make him extremely fruitful and multiply his descendants. He will become the father of twelve princes, and I will make him a great nation. But my covenant will be confirmed with Isaac, who will be born to you and Sarah about this time next year" (Genesis 17:15-21 NLT).

Interesting to see that both Abraham and Sarah laugh in disbelief. Nevertheless, that was promise number seven!

Then one of them said, "I will return to you about this time next year, and your wife, Sarah, will have a son!..." (Genesis 18:10 NLT).

The angels come…promise number eight.

Abraham and Sarah were both very old by this time, and Sarah was long past the age of having children. So she laughed silently to herself and said, "How could a worn-out woman like me enjoy such pleasure, especially when my master—my husband—is also so old?" Then the Lord said to Abraham, "Why did Sarah laugh? Why did she say, 'Can an old woman like me have a baby?' Is anything too hard for the Lord? I will return about this time next year, and Sarah will have a son" (Genesis 18:11-14 NLT).

For Abraham will certainly become a great and mighty nation, and all the nations of the earth will be blessed through him. I have singled him out so that he will direct his sons and their families to keep the way of the Lord by doing what is right and just. Then I will do for Abraham all that I have promised (Genesis 18:18-19 NLT).

That is promise number nine.

Nine promises—Isaac is born when Abraham is 100 years old. Promise fulfilled!

So, what do we see? Twenty-five years of struggle. We see a man who needs constant reassuring. He obviously doubts God's faithfulness, protection, and integrity. He lies, is rather selfish, and grossly impatient. I am sure you would agree that he doesn't pass for a father of our faith!

Yet Paul writes:

(As it is written, I have made thee a father of many nations,) before him whom he believed, even God, who quickeneth the dead, and calleth those things which be not as though they were. Who against hope believed in hope, that he might become the father of many nations, according to that which was spoken, So shall thy seed be. And being not weak in faith, he considered not his own body now dead, when he was about an hundred years old, neither yet the deadness of Sarah's womb: He staggered not at the promise of God through unbelief; but was strong in faith, giving glory to God; and being fully persuaded that, what he had promised, he was able also to perform (Romans 4:17-21).

Does that first verse in the Scripture passage sound accurate to you? It sounds the exact opposite, doesn't it? And how about, *"Who against hope believed in hope…"* Umm…did he really?

"And being not weak in faith..." Seriously? We see weakness throughout the story, right?

"He staggered not at the promise of God through unbelief..." Hmmm, what about Eliezer and Hagar?

"But was strong in faith. And being fully persuaded that, what he had promised, he was able also to perform...." This is all wrong, isn't it?

Then the clincher... *"And because of Abraham's faith, God counted him as righteous"* (Romans 4:22 NLT).

Here is my conclusion: Once we get into a position of faith, God absolutely forgets all that it takes us to get there.

And I will forgive their wickedness, and I will never again remember their sins (Hebrews 8:12 NLT).

God, blots out our doubt, unbelief, and the remembrance of sin. Once Abraham lines up, God is like, "That's it, son! I don't remember your transgressions; I don't remember you pimping out your wife! In fact, generations will remember you as faithful, strong, steadfast, unwavering, and ever-hopeful."

Finishing is infinitely more important than starting.

Herein is the *Test of Success*: Can you reconcile your history with your destiny? Do you keep hearing failure, failure...looser, looser...nobody, faker, pretender—or do you hear servant, minister, *huperetes*? Have you become bitter, cynical, or critical because of the myriad of betrayals and backstabbing? Papa Kurt, like you and I, must decide whether to become jaded from his 10,000 missteps or remain childlike about his amazing journey of faith.

Friend, unless you thoroughly reconcile your history, you will either mute or distort God's voice. You will either minister from your wound or His manifested grace and mercy. Warning: Oftentimes the voice of your broken history will sound just like the voice of God.

The Test of Success forces us to ponder:

- What if I do build that church?
- What if I do get renowned?
- What if I actually become a best-selling author?
- What if I build a global ministry?
- What if I really raise a dead child back to life?
- What if I write the next Christian pop hit?
- What if it really starts to work?

The real question is: Can you keep your soul or will you lose it at the altar of success?

BOASTING

So I repeat. Let no one think that I'm a fool. But if you do, at least show me the patience you would show a fool, so that I too may boast a little. Of course, what I'm about to tell you is not with the Lord's authority, but as a "fool." For since many love to boast about their worldly achievements, allow me the opportunity to join them (2 Corinthians 11:16-18 TPT).

Paul basically says that "They are impressing you with a lot of resumes. Here is mine. Since you are impressed by these things, let me tell you what I have done:

Are these "super-apostles" of yours Hebrews? I am too. Are they Israelites? So am I. Are they descendants of Abraham? Me too! Are they servants of the Anointed One? I'm beside myself when I speak this way, but I am much more of a servant than they. I have worked much harder for God, taken more beatings, and been dragged to more prisons than they. I've been flogged excessively, multiple times, even to the point of death. Five times I've received thirty-nine lashes from the Jewish leaders. Three times I experienced being beaten with rods. Once they stoned me. Three times I've been shipwrecked; for an entire night and a day I was adrift in the open sea. In my difficult travels I've faced many dangerous situations: perilous rivers, robbers, foreigners, and even my own people. I've survived deadly peril in the city, in the wilderness, with storms at sea, and with spies posing as believers. I've toiled to the point of exhaustion and gone through many sleepless nights. I've frequently been deprived of food and water, left hungry and shivering out in the cold, lacking proper clothing. And besides these painful circumstances, I have the daily pressure of my responsibility for all the churches, with a deep concern weighing heavily on my heart for their welfare. I am not aloof, for who is desperate and weak and I do not feel their weakness? Who is led astray into sin and I do not burn with zeal to restore him? If boasting is necessary, I will boast about examples of my weakness" (2 Corinthians 11:22-30 TPT).

Can you imagine someone saying that they have served God harder than Paul? This is how he solidifies his credentials:

1. Lashes: Remember those lashes Jesus received… once? Paul had five times more.

2. Rods: This punishment was so severe that prisoners sometimes never walked again.

3. Stoning: Rarely did anyone recover from a stoning. In fact, the executioners didn't stop until the convict was believed to be dead!

4. Peril: Insurmountable pressure from all sides…

Bottom line, Paul does not pride himself in victories and accomplishments, or success and elevation, but boasts in moments of humbling, pain, peril, and brokenness—*"because of my love for Christ—I am made yet stronger. For my weakness becomes a portal to God's power"* (2 Corinthians 12:10 TPT).

In as much as I have enjoyed undeserved elevation, it is not the crowds, limousines, or notoriety that qualifies me to serve in the capacity that I do. Rather, it is the bug-infested rooms, the expired food, the attempted poisonings, gunfire, betrayals, languor, and exhaustion.

While many a young man or woman is attracted to the ministry because of the trappings of fame and financial success, Paul teaches us something that we best be advised to embrace. Cherish your humble moments. That is what actually qualifies you to become a voice in the life of another. My sufferings are the reason I am writing this book for you. I have endured much and passed many a test. Whether history will consider me successful is irrelevant. I am a *huperetes*.

Let me sign off with Paul's desperate admonition to the elders of the church in Ephesus:

But whether I live or die is not important, for I don't esteem my life as indispensable. It's more important for me to fulfill my destiny and to finish the ministry my Lord Jesus has assigned to me, which is to faithfully preach the wonderful news of God's grace. I've been a part of your lives and shared with you many times the message of God's kingdom realm. But now I leave you, and you will not see my face again. If any of you should be lost, I will not be blamed, for my conscience is clean, because I've taught you everything I could about God's eternal plan and I've held nothing back. So guard your hearts. Be true shepherds over all the flock and feed them well. Remember, it was the Holy Spirit who appointed you to guard and oversee the churches that belong to Jesus, the Anointed One, which he purchased and established by his own blood. I know that after I leave, imposters who have no loyalty to the flock will come among you like savage wolves. Even some from among your very own ranks will rise up, twisting the truth to seduce people into following them instead of Jesus (Acts 20:24-30 TPT).

Epilogue

Prior to the great flood, God would hydrate the ground with dew every morning.

> *The Lord saw how great the wickedness of the human race had become on the earth, and that every inclination of the thoughts of the human heart was only evil all the time. The Lord regretted that he had made human beings on the earth, and his heart was deeply troubled. So the Lord said, "I will wipe from the face of the earth the human race I have created—and with them the animals, the birds and the creatures that move along the ground—for I regret that I have made them"* (Genesis 6:5-7 NIV).

To paraphrase, God basically says to Noah, "Son, I am disgusted by evil. I need to hit reset on My creation plan. I am going to send this thing called "rain." I know you've never seen it before, but it will destroy everything. So, I want you to build me a very big vessel where people and other living creatures will shelter."

If you read this through the theological prism of contemporary Christendom, you'll miss a lot. This is an absurd instruction. And here is why. First, Noah had never seen rain or a boat before. Reminds you of the *Test of Faith*, doesn't it? Imagine the start of this massive project. The materials and labor needed to house countless species of animals must have been huge. Imagine the first couple of years…

Okay, I think Noah is my greatest hero of faith. He had such absurd faith. Can you imagine his explanation to his kinfolk and his people? "Okay guys, something huge is coming. It's called RAIN!"

"What do you mean, rain?"

Imagine the building process. I can imagine one of his sons asking, "Papa, are you sure about these measurements?"

"Yep…that's what God said."

"What is rain again?"

"I don't know, son. Let's just build it. We will find out when the time comes."

Imagine those conversations for one hundred and twenty years! The grit it would take to persevere. Talk about the *Test of Conviction!* God does not tell Noah that it would take him twelve decades to complete the assignment. Can you imagine year forty?

When the ark is ready, God says, "Okay, now go call them in!"

And of course, the people in the neighborhood are mocking Noah and smearing him. The man of God is a laughingstock to a community that thinks he has gone absolutely bonkers. But guess who would have the last laugh? Noah!

When God calls us to ministry, our natural response is typically, "Umm…yes, of course, Lord…but where to? What to? When to? How to?" And then the silence, the deafening silence of almighty God as He waits for you to respond. The immaculate invitation is so absurd, so vague, so blurry, so foggy that it forever rattles us to the core. Enter the *Test of Faith!* Everyone who serves God must to pass this first test. He asks us, "Will you serve Me without knowing the details? Can you say yes to a proposition that burns inside of you, without fully understanding it?" That is where most people stop, yet that is the beginning of all ministry—the foggy invitation to go where you have never been.

So you say yes to launching a ministry, volunteering in that department, etc. Then suddenly the kids fall sick, your family doesn't like it, your body starts acting up, finances are tight.… Suddenly everything is wrong. So you ask God, "Lord, can we go back to the way we were?" You retreat. You are facing the *Test of Conviction.* Many of us retreat to that place of invitation. We seek to rehash the emotions of the call, the proverbial good old days!

"Lord," you protest, "I'm going to continue because You are by my side. Your work burns within me. Returning to yesterday is simply not an option." Peace floods your heart. You are a *huperetes,* a servant in God's Kingdom doing God's dream!

Suddenly, your friends don't understand why you are so committed. They seem to be bothered by your passion and begin to criticize you.

"Ooh, so you are going on another mission trip?"

"Wow, what does your family think about all these hours at church?"

"You don't seem balanced, man…too much ministry bro!"

Welcome to the *Test of Isolation*. The test reveals just how much we rely on human affirmation. We all need company, but be wary of an addiction to cheerleaders. The test demands that you unwaveringly answer these questions: Will I go alone? Am I okay if everyone deserts me? It is 2 a.m. and you are thinking, *What am I doing here? Do I have to do this? Do I have to be this intense?*

It is at the place of isolation where God begins to bring out what's inside you. It is where He begins to talk to you, to give you revelation, to separate you from the crowd. In the place of isolation, you find *you*. There is no fanfare, no drums, no crowds, no music…just you and the harsh wilderness.

Then you come out saying things a little different from what your pastor or mentor say. Your old crowd begins to protest: "Huh? Who do you think you are? Just because you have been fasting, pressing in a little bit you think you are all of that?" They begin to trample over you. Sit down friend, this is the *Test of Servanthood*. Will you keep going, keep rowing even when no one really sees you?

So you pass that test and you begin to zealously serve Jesus. You want to go where others don't even think about going. Your peers begin to feel threatened. They start looking for things to criticize about you. Some even lay traps in your path. You are leaving them behind, and they do not like that. "At this rate, he will soon be teaching us," they protest. Some develop a sense of mission to put you "back in your place" where they know how to relate to you. Resist, and they will crush you. Here is the evolution—they will first ignore you, then they will treat you like dirt, and ultimately, they attack. This is the *Test of Reputation*. "What if God wants me to pull back until the attacks stop?" you might ask. Here is an inconvenient truth—you cannot minister effectively if you are addicted to applause.

Now I must say that the need for affirmation and significance is a basic psychological need. We all like to be liked. But minister, you better deal with that really fast and very decisively. Will you serve Jesus even though they do not like you? Can you drink of the cup of persecution like your Savior and Lord did?

Remember, you may cry, your pillow may be wet with tears every night, but in the morning, you will *hupereteo* yet again. You are a *huperetes*. It matters not whether you are liked or not, but that you do His bidding.

Pass this test and the weariness of the journey starts to work on you. You wonder, *How long can I take these attacks? How long can I endure isolation from my family and friends? What if I just end up alone? What am I going to do for retirement? Ministry doesn't pay much.* Waiting and the passage of time begin to work on you. Welcome to the *Test of Time*. Will you keep going, keep rowing after the sun sets?

Push and voila...they call you successful. But the more urgent question is: Will you like Moses lead God's people out of Israel but fail to enter the Promised Land? Will you like Noah build the ark, but lose control to inebriation and lack of dignity? Will you like Samson slay hundreds by your extraordinary might, but die blind? Will you like Solomon be the wisest of all men, yet end up marrying foreign women and worshipping their gods? Will you pass the *Test of Success?*

I was trying to persuade an important government official to trust God for her future when I clearly heard the Lord say, "Ask her: Do I have to repeat myself?" She knew exactly what the Lord meant. She eventually broke through, which reminded me of Abraham. God had to repeat Himself nine times because

Abraham just doesn't get it. So I ask the same question: "Does God have to repeat Himself?"

You may have heard God but because of trepidation and persecution, isolation, pressure, and the smears, you are second guessing what you have heard. You saw it clearly, but now it is blurry and you want God to speak to you "clearly" again.

Everyone who will read this book has multiplied times more knowledge than our first century counterparts. The irony is we are doing a whole lot less. Most of us are addicted to knowing more, attending conferences, viewing clips, showing up at Bible studies, gathering information and more and more knowledge instead of executing. We are learning but failing to take action.

> *...From everyone to whom much has been given, much will be required; and to whom they entrusted much, of him they will ask all the more* (Luke 12:48 AMP).

I have been blessed beyond anything I would have ever dreamed. I am the boy who grew up in an impoverished country with death on the doorstep. My salvation was a divine interruption to what would have been a disastrously short life filled with struggle. But God... God called me to serve Him and gifted me with spiritual endowments for what has been an incredible ministry journey. I am not special by any means. It is true when I say that because God did it for me, He can most assuredly do it for you.

I believe that we stand at the periphery of a new dispensation of radical ministry. As we examine new ways to build God's Kingdom, may we never forget who we really are. That we are under-rowers called to *hupereteo*—row...row...row...until our days are done. May we become.

About the Author

Dennis Sempebwa is the founder and president of Eagle's Wings International, an apostolic missionary organization with hubs in twenty-six countries. He serves as the founder and chancellor of THE 300, an accredited, 21st century, ministry training college that trains believers in multiple countries. Dennis is also the president and CEO of The Sahara Wisdom Center, a multinational training corporation committed to inspiring transformational thinking in academia, private institutions, and governments.

Dubbed one of Africa's new breed of top pragmatic leaders, Dennis has served in eighty countries and authored fourteen books. He is a Global Goodwill Ambassador and a highly sought-after speaker who holds numerous doctorate degrees.

Dennis has been married to his beloved wife, Ingrid, for twenty-four years. They are blessed with five children: Adam, Abigail, Caleb, Judah, and Elijah. They currently reside in the great state of Texas in the USA.

Contact Information

Dr. Dennis D. Sempebwa
President & Founder
Eagle's Wings International

President & Chancellor
THE 300

Website: www.the300.com
McKinney, Texas, USA

Get in touch with us:
EAGLE'S WINGS INTERNATIONAL

PO Box 6295, McKinney TX 75071, USA
Email: office@e-wings.net

 /ddsempebwa

 /drdennissempebwa

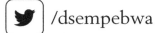 /dsempebwa

 /in/dennis-sempebwa-d-min-phd

Made in the USA
Coppell, TX
22 August 2020

34002061R00085